PRIVATE NOTEBOOKS

28.1.15.

29.1.15.

30.1.15.

31.1.15.

PRIVATE
NOTEBOOKS

1914–1916

LUDWIG
WITTGENSTEIN

Edited and Translated by
Marjorie Perloff

LIVERIGHT PUBLISHING CORPORATION

A Division *of* W. W. Norton *&* Company

Independent Publishers Since 1923

For information about permission to reproduce selections from this book,
write to Permissions, Liveright Publishing Corporation, a division of
W. W. Norton & Company, Inc., 500 Fifth Avenue, New York, NY 10110

For information about special discounts for bulk purchases, please contact
W. W. Norton Special Sales at specialsales@wwnorton.com or 800-233-4830

Manufacturing by Lake Book Manufacturing
Book design by Marysarah Quinn
Production manager: Anna Oler

ISBN 978-1-324-09080-9

Liveright Publishing Corporation
500 Fifth Avenue
New York, N.Y. 10110
www.wwnorton.com

W. W. Norton & Company Ltd.
15 Carlisle Street
London W1D 3BS

1 2 3 4 5 6 7 8 9 0

For Daniel Herwitz,

with whom I first read Wittgenstein

CONTENTS

A NOTE ON THE TRANSLATION
AND TRANSCRIPTION

WITTGENSTEIN'S MAJOR WRITINGS have generally been published in bilingual editions that have the German and English on facing pages. Wittgenstein wrote in his native German all his life, and because language is so central to his concerns, it is important to be able to read the English version against the German. Then, too, there is currently no German edition of the *Private Notebooks 1914–1916*, and so this edition can also satisfy the needs of the German-speaking reader who has little English. The footnotes appearing here in the notebooks are given in English only to avoid repetition.

In translating Wittgenstein's text, I have tried, as much as possible, to reproduce Wittgenstein's colloquial Austro-German phrasing, idiom, and syntax. In these diaries, Wittgenstein largely writes the way he talks—abruptly, informally, concretely, and often with telling metaphor, as in "I am like a burnt-out oven, full of slag and dung."

The recto passages cited were originally translated for the 1961 edition of *Notebooks 1914–1916* by Wittgenstein's great disciple and executor, G. E. [Elizabeth] M. Anscombe. This translation, now more than sixty years old, struck me as inadequate, and I have retranslated the cited passages here.

———

WITTGENSTEIN WROTE his "private" notes in code on the left (verso) pages of each notebook and the philosophical entries—an embryo version of the *Tractatus Logico-Philosophicus*—uncoded on the right (recto) pages. The text of the verso pages was carefully decoded by a team of editors working at the University of Bergen to produce the *Nachlass*. This edition reproduces, as faithfully as possible, this decoded manuscript, following Wittgenstein's own layout and spacing. The reader will want to note the following:

1. Each entry is dated; I have moved the dates from the right side of each page (as occurred in the original) to the left side for easier access. Each date, transcribed in European style— 8.10.14 is October 8, 1914—appears directly above the entry itself for easy cross-reference with the German on the facing page.

2. Reproducing Wittgenstein's punctuation is not always easy because, aside from the constant flow of exclamation points and question marks, there are, occasionally in Notebook 1 and pervasively in Notebook 2, dashes of different lengths. In an essay titled "Wittgenstein's Gebetsstriche" ("Wittgenstein's Prayer Lines"), Martin Pilch has argued that the long dashes (for example, — or — — or even — — — and sometimes followed by an equal sign, =) represent forms of

prayer. His argument is convincing, but it is still not clear precisely what particular dashes signify. And in Notebook 3, they have disappeared completely. I have reproduced these dashes as accurately as possible, just to give the feel of this curious form of punctuation.

3. As I was editing the notebooks, it occurred to me that the short Notebook 3 would make much more sense if I included some of the most striking and beautiful passages from the philosophical side (the recto); indeed, as I argue throughout, verso and recto, at first quite disconnected, gradually come together so that, by the end, they often correspond. This does not mean neat pairing of any sort, but a close and uncanny chronological correspondence between the left-hand and right-hand pages.

   All recto entries are presented in italic font; all verso entries are presented in Roman font so that the distinction will be clear.

4. The numbers in brackets in the italicized entries are cross-references, as given in the text of the published *Notebooks 1914–1916*, to the *Tractatus* where the same statement will often appear with slightly different wording.

5. It is customary to cite Wittgenstein's *Tractatus* and *Philosophical Investigations*, both written in short, aphoristic paragraphs, by paragraph entry (§), not page. I follow this usage here.

––––––––––

THE MANUSCRIPT NOTEBOOKS 101, 102, and 103 are in the Wren Library at Trinity College, Cambridge. Copyright: The Master and Fellows of Trinity College, Cambridge. Copyright in transcription of the German original: University of Bergen, Bergen. All rights reserved.

The text found here reproduces the latest and most authoritative Bergen edition of Wittgenstein's three notebooks, known as the Bergen Nachlass Edition (BNE) and found at http://wittgensteinsource .org and http://wittgensteinonline.no/.

PRIVATE NOTEBOOKS

INTRODUCTION

T HROUGHOUT HIS LIFE, Ludwig Wittgenstein, arguably the most important philosopher of the twentieth century, contemplated suicide, and yet on his deathbed he said to his landlady, "Tell them I've had a wonderful life."[1] Wittgenstein was as mysterious and contradictory as a character in a Dostoevsky novel or a play by Harold Pinter.

Born into one of the wealthiest families in what was then the Austro-Hungarian Empire—his father was an iron and steel magnate and great patron of the arts—Wittgenstein, in the wake of World War I, gave away his entire fortune to his siblings, wanting to be free of the obligations money imposes. From then on, he lived an ascetic life, first as a village schoolmaster in lower Austria, later in his sparsely furnished Cambridge rooms or in his tiny mountain cottage in Norway. Yet this confirmed anti-materialist designed for his sister Gretl in Vienna a starkly beautiful modernist house and attended to every detail of its elaborate and costly construction from radiators to doorknobs.

The contradictions multiply. Wittgenstein came from a Jewish family—his great-grandfather Moses Meier, a land agent, took on the name Wittgenstein from his employers—but was baptized at birth into the Catholic Church and later displayed strong leanings toward Protestant piety. He disliked organized religion but loved the Gospels, whose parables and proverbs he knew by heart. In a highly original critique of James Frazer's *Golden Bough*, Wittgenstein argued that the early vegetation myths Frazer regarded as "primitive" must be understood as specific *practices*, in which case they were perfectly reasonable; indeed, to study religion as a *practice*, he argued, is to understand that no one religion can be superior to any other. Yet the Jewish religion was somehow excluded from this tolerant assessment: Wittgenstein never quite shook off the residual anti-Semitism of his wholly secularized upper-class Viennese milieu and actually remarked at one point that Jews (himself included) could not be original thinkers.

At Cambridge, where he taught from 1929 until 1947, Wittgenstein became something of a legend, and yet he was anything but an academic philosopher. Trained as an engineer, he often remarked that he had never read Aristotle or Descartes. His Cambridge world was almost exclusively male, and yet his favorite student was Elizabeth Anscombe—Wittgenstein called her "an honorary man"—who became his first important translator, editor, and the chief executor of his literary estate. Wittgenstein's Cambridge lectures, recorded (at that time in shorthand) by his most devoted disciples, were widely published, but he continued to do his philosophical writing in German, declaring that only his native language would do, although—another paradox—he had little desire to spend time in his native country, finding even his annual Christmas visits to his family difficult, if not painful. But the distance between himself and his Viennese past did not mean that he felt at home in England; on the contrary, he repeatedly told colleagues and students that he was an alien among them and, at one point in the mid-1930s, contemplated a move to the then Soviet Union where he hoped to become an ordinary manual worker.

No doubt, this alienation had something to do with his homosexuality. Three of Wittgenstein's older brothers, all three probably homosexual, as was Ludwig, had committed suicide. In the Vienna of the early twentieth century, "deviant" sexuality could not be discussed openly; even Freud, after all, regarded homosexuality, whose manifestations were entirely illegal, as a disease that could be cured. British laws were similarly strict, but in intellectual Cambridge, there was less constraint, and Wittgenstein could be more open about his feelings, first for David Pinsent, later for Francis Skinner, and finally for Ben Richards.

At the same time, Wittgenstein himself had a contrary streak when it came to his gay colleagues. When, in 1912, his good friend, the soon-to-be famous economist John Maynard Keynes, himself gay, proposed him for the exclusive "Apostles" club, Wittgenstein soon resigned because he could not abide the open and endless gossip about sex. The same thing happened later with the Bloomsbury set: Wittgenstein declared himself appalled by Lytton Strachey's minute accounts of his sexual liaisons—especially, as was the case in Bloomsbury, in the presence of female members such as Vanessa Bell and Virginia Woolf.

A queer—Wittgenstein frequently uses the adjective "queer," although in his day the word simply meant "odd" (or did it?)—who did not approve of his fellow queers, just as he was a Jew who was critical of Jews; in this respect, Wittgenstein resembled his contemporary Marcel Proust. But whereas Proust was a passionate modernist, who championed the new music, art, and theater of his time, Wittgenstein, who adored Mozart and Beethoven and participated eagerly in the avid music-making that took place at the Palais Wittgenstein in his youth, refused to have anything to do with composers later than Brahms and would walk out of a concert hall if the orchestra was playing a Richard Strauss concerto or a Mahler symphony. The same is true for his taste in literature, which was for the German classics—Goethe, Heine, Gottfried Keller, the Austrian Franz Grillparzer. In his long years in England, he seems never to have read the Romantics or Jane Austen or his modernist contemporaries. Indeed, Wittgenstein insisted that Goethe was greater than Shakespeare, whose characters, created in the long-ago sixteenth century, he considered too remote, whereas Goethe's thoughts and feelings were ones that could, he felt, be shared by all.

A further anomaly: Wittgenstein, who had not the slightest use for the avant-garde, was himself nothing if not an avant-gardist. His writings avoid all conventional argumentation or plotting—beginning, middle, and end—and rely on aphorism, anecdote, conceit, collage, and fragment. He regularly numbered his short paragraphs, and in the *Tractatus Logico-Philosophicus* itself he devised an elaborate mathematical system that takes us from 3.001 to 3.01, 3.02, 3.03, 3.031 and so on. The combination of numerical precision and aphoristic, enigmatic statement is reminiscent of another of his contemporaries, Marcel Duchamp, whose readymades and other works of art Wittgenstein would have surely found "too ridiculous for words."[2] Duchamp, in his turn, knew nothing of Wittgenstein, but such of his disciples as Jasper Johns and John Cage became ardent readers of the *Philosophical Investigations* and *Culture and Value*.

Here we witness the central paradox that makes Wittgenstein so unique. This austere, intellectually demanding, and often intolerant member of the Viennese upper class came to insist that philosophy was by no means a special discipline with its own meta-language and "scientific" method but, on the contrary, a practice, relying on commonsense solutions and the conviction that "ordinary language is alright."[3] If, as first articulated in the war notebook of 1915, "the *limits of my language* mean the limits of my world,"[4] the language in question is the language we use in our everyday communication. "*The limits of my language* mean the limits of my world" because, for Wittgenstein, "Language is not *contiguous* to anything else."[5] We don't, as is generally thought, *first* have thoughts and *then* put those thoughts into words; we simply use words. *There are no thoughts outside of language.* We can begin to understand this axiom if we pose a question such as "Why can't a dog simulate pain? Is he too honest?"[6]

The *Philosophical Investigations* opens with a critique of Augustine's view in the *Confessions* that children learn the meaning of words by pointing at objects or persons: *apple, orange, table, tree, Mommy*. But most words—*and, of, their, without, must, even, feel, see*—are not nouns that name things or persons at all, and yet we quickly learn to use them. A three-year-old, for example, might well say, "I hope it won't rain tomorrow," but if you asked her what the word *hope* means, she would not be able to give you a meaningful definition. Rather, having heard adults use the word *hope* often enough, she would know where it goes in a sentence.

What is central to language, accordingly, is not matching names and things, but grammar—the way words are actually put together in a given phrase or sentence. Grammar is neither good or bad, right or wrong, it is merely descriptive. Hence, "There are no gaps in grammar; grammar is always complete." Or, as Wittgenstein quipped, "In philosophy all that is not gas is grammar."[7] And hence the famous sentence in the *Philosophical Investigations*, "*The meaning of a word is its use in the language.*"[8] And that use is astonishingly variable.

The understanding of *context* is, for Wittgenstein, at the heart of understanding how language works and especially the language of poetry. Perhaps poets, artists, composers, and filmmakers have taken such a special interest in Wittgenstein because they recognize that he is himself a kind of conceptual poet. "I believe I summed up," he wrote in 1933, "where I stand in relation to philosophy when I said that philosophy could only be written as a form of poetry" ("*Philosophie dürfte man eigentlich nur dichten*").[9] The German verb *dichten* refers to any kind of imaginative writing—fiction and drama as well as lyric poetry. What Wittgenstein means here is that for him, "philosophy" is not, as is conventionally thought, some kind of abstract theory whether of truth (metaphysics) or knowledge (epistemology) or of ethics, but an *activity*—not something one *knows* but something one *does*. "Philosophy is the attempt to be rid of a particular kind of puzzlement" by means of language. "Instinctively we use language rightly; but to the intellect this use is a puzzle."[10] The philosopher's aim—as Wittgenstein put it in a now famous aphorism—is thus "To show the fly the way out of the fly-bottle."[11]

As a poetry critic, the puzzles of language have always been my own passion. Perhaps it is, at least in part, the passion of exiles—those of us who must learn to negotiate the world in a language not originally our own. As a refugee from Hitler's Vienna in 1938, I have always felt a special affinity for such Wittgenstein puzzles as "When I say that the orders 'Bring me sugar' and 'Bring me milk' make sense, but not the combination 'Milk me sugar,' that does not mean that the utterance of this combination of words has no effect."[12] A poet, after all, might want to use the phrase "Milk me sugar" for special reasons. In Gertrude Stein's poem "Sacred Emily," for example, we find the line "Egg be takers," which sounds merely nonsensical until we consider its place among the poem's sexual innuendoes. "Egg be takers," for example, plays on the words *eggbeaters*, *betake*, and so on. "Sometimes," said Wittgenstein, "you have to take an expression out of the language, to send it for cleaning, —& then you can put it back in circulation."[13] And again, "The only way to do philosophy is to do everything twice."[14]

———

To do everything twice: This prescription provides a perfect entrance into the three *Private Notebooks*, translated here for the first time. Written during the early years of World War I, when Wittgenstein was serving as an infantryman on the Eastern Front, they present his own difficult and often painful transition from doing philosophy for the first time to doing it over again. For these *notebooks* track the movement whereby their author, slowly and with no prior intention, came to transform what began as a rigorous treatise on logic—a treatise that would provide answers to some of the most pressing problems as to the status of propositions and their "truth functions"—into a much larger, more profound discussion of ethics and aesthetics, indeed the meaning of life and death.

Wittgenstein was only twenty-five when he enlisted in the Austrian army on August 7, 1914, just a day after the Austro-Hungarian Empire had declared war on Russia and six weeks after the assassination of the Archduke Ferdinand at Sarajevo—the event that absurdly triggered the Great War. It was, to say the least, an odd decision. For one thing, Wittgenstein had a medical deferment because of a hernia. More important: He had never exhibited the slightest interest in politics or expressed patriotic sentiments. Indeed, he had been living, for the previous five years, in the nation that was to be Austria's most powerful enemy—England, first in Manchester, where he studied aeronautics, and then in Cambridge, where he went to study logic with Bertrand Russell, whose *Principia Mathematica* had aroused his interest. In Cambridge, he also made friends with the philosopher G. E. Moore and the afore-mentioned John Maynard Keynes, and it was at one of Russell's "squashes" (social evenings) that he met the young math student named David Pinsent, who became the object of his love, although their relationship evidently remained platonic. The two traveled to Iceland together in the summer of 1912, to Norway in 1913, and were planning another holiday (Spain? the Hebrides?) together in early August 1914 when the outbreak of war abruptly changed their plans. They were never to see one another again: Pinsent, though not in the military, was killed in an aeronautical accident in 1918. He was twenty-seven.

In the first of the three extant notebooks (August 9, 1914–October 30, 1914), Wittgenstein narrates the daily misery of serv-ing on a patrol ship, the *Goplana*, that made its way up and down the Vistula River from Kraków to the small towns then part of Galicia. The army tasks were arduous enough, but the constant ref-erences to "my work" refer to Wittgenstein's own work—the trea-tise on logic he had been writing for the previous year, designed as a corrective to the work of his mentors, Bertrand Russell and Gottlob Frege. In the early war years, he developed what is known as the picture theory of language, which held that elements of a proposition are arranged so as to stand for the objects they depict.

But the picture theory proved to be limiting, for Wittgenstein was soon recognizing that "true" propositions are either tautologies ("Either it is raining or it is not raining") or belong to the realm of science and mathematics. All other propositions are contingent: They make statements that cannot be proven. What, then, was the value of traditional "logic"?

By the winter of 1914–1915, when Wittgenstein was stationed in the artillery workshop at Kraków, he found it more and more difficult to do any of his own work: he was totally blocked. On January 13, 1915, for example, he writes that his thoughts themselves were "tired" (*müde*): "It is as if a flame had been extinguished and I must wait till it begins to burn again of its own accord." Repeatedly, he was searching for what he called *the redeeming word* (*das erlösende Wort*)—a key principle that would somehow resolve his philosophical quandaries. The redeeming word, in this context, calls to mind the opening lines of the Gospel of St. John: "In the beginning was the Word, / And the Word was with God, / And the Word was God"—the *Logos*. But in the course of these war months, a kind of dark night of the soul, Wittgenstein discovered that there is no "redeeming word," no unitary Logos that supplies us with solutions to the basic questions of human life. He came to learn that there are no answers, only questions.

It was, as the notebooks testify, an arduous process. Wittgenstein began to write his "war notebook" on August 9, 1914. For the entries of any single day in each notebook, his personal remarks, written in a code he had learned and used with his siblings when he was young,* are placed on the left-hand page (the verso). On

---

* The code is a fairly simple reversal of the alphabet Wittgenstein evidently used with his siblings when they were children: z = a, y = b, x = c, and so on. Wittgenstein was to use it again in the 1930s. Ilse Somavilla has found some 450 coded remarks in the whole corpus.

the right-hand page (the recto), he composed, in normal script, the logical treatise that was to be the penultimate draft of the *Tractatus Logico-Philosophicus* (1922). Thus, the entries for any single day were written on a two-page (verso-recto) spread.

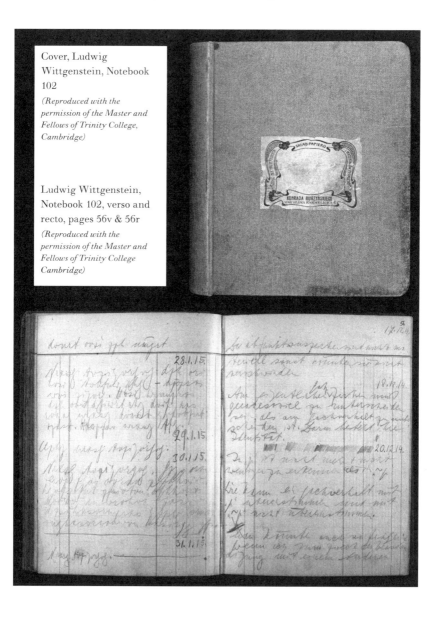

Cover, Ludwig Wittgenstein, Notebook 102

(Reproduced with the permission of the Master and Fellows of Trinity College, Cambridge)

Ludwig Wittgenstein, Notebook 102, verso and recto, pages 56v & 56r

(Reproduced with the permission of the Master and Fellows of Trinity College Cambridge)

The right-hand pages were published as early as 1961 and are available today in a bilingual edition under the title *Notebooks 1914–1916.** But the left-hand, or "secret," pages have never been published in English, and there is not even an authoritative text in German. How could such an omission occur? I take up that question later in the Afterword. Here, let me just make clear that there are evidently at least three missing notebooks: The first, as we can see, would have covered the nine-month hiatus between June 22, 1915 and March 28 (?), 1916. The others would have continued the story that breaks off with the last private entry on August 19, 1916, detailing the final months of the war and Wittgenstein's year as a prisoner of war in Cassino, Italy. Unfortunately, these notebooks were lost.

The surviving notebooks are remarkable for their candor, their self-criticism, their sexual preoccupations, and their dark humor. Despite the paradoxes and contradictions I have been detailing, Wittgenstein was quite consistent in one respect. It was his aim, throughout his life, *to turn into a different person.*[15] Others might want to change the government, the political order, a particular institution or industry. Wittgenstein had no interest in such external institutions; his sole aim was to change himself. And it was the war with all its challenges and difficulties that allowed him to do so. By the summer of 1916, when the secret diary breaks off, Wittgenstein had come to the conclusion that "The sense of the world must lie outside the world," that *in the world*, "everything is as it is and happens as it does happen."[16] Hence, as the Conclusion to the *Tractatus* famously puts it, "Of what one cannot speak, of that one must be silent."[17]

---

* The most recent edition of *Notebooks 1914–1916* dates from 1979, more than forty years ago.

The appeal of Wittgenstein's philosophy has everything to do with what *cannot be said*. His is not an admonition to keep silent about our deepest feelings—he is no Freud—but rather, because language is central to his concerns, to beware of making generalizations and claiming to know "the truth" about this or that aspect of life. Were Wittgenstein alive today, he would be questioning such buzzwords as *systemic* and *intersectionality* and would cringe at the current use of the word *science*, as in that absurd imperative of the airwaves, "Just follow the science." Does *science* mean one thing? And isn't it ironic that the word *science* is now ubiquitously applied to *medicine*, which, as physicians themselves have always admitted, must be regarded as hardly an exact science, indeed to some extent an "art." Then, too, Wittgenstein would have asked, whose science is the authoritative one? And how does one know?

"Hegel," Wittgenstein once remarked to a friend, "seems to me to be always wanting to say that things which look different are really the same. Whereas my interest is in showing that things which look the same are really different."[18] It is the uncanny understanding of *difference*—a kind of negative theology—that makes Wittgenstein's aphoristic and enigmatic philosophical writings so special. Nothing is ever taken for granted. "Why can't my right hand give my left hand money?" we read in the *Philosophical Investigations*, "My right hand can put it into my left hand. . . . But the further practical consequences would not be those of a gift."[19] Here Wittgenstein is literalizing the common metaphoric idiom, "The left hand doesn't know what the right hand is doing," showing how misleading language can be. Or again, "You can't hear God speak to someone else, you can hear him only if you are being addressed."[20]

In such aphoristic exempla, we see Wittgenstein questioning

the use of the most ordinary words: *give* in the first instance, *hear* in the second. It was in the war notebooks, in which Wittgenstein records his painful relationships with others—at one point, he fears a duel—that these hard questions begin to be asked. Once the single "redemptive word" is no longer sought, the doors of perception open, and what is remarkable is that verso and recto in the notebooks—the private and the public—begin to correspond to one another: This edition allows us to see this for the first time. Whereas, in the early notebooks, the recto is full of mathematical equations used in symbolic logic and the verso details trivial daily events, especially relating to Wittgenstein's animosity toward his fellow soldiers, on July 7, 1916, a day before the recto contains the sentence, "To believe in a God means to see that the facts of the world are not the end of the matter," on the verso we read, set down on the page as a poetic couplet:

> But the connection will have been made!
> What cannot be said, <u>cannot</u> be said!

> [*Aber die Verbindung wird hergestellt werden!*
> *Was sich nicht sagen läßt, <u>läßt</u> sich nicht sagen!*]

Here is the first version of *Tractatus* 7: "Of what one cannot speak, of that one must be silent," cited earlier.

But, as the personal diary entries reveal, Wittgenstein could not remain on this lofty plane. The very last private entry we have in Notebook 3—19.8.16 (written shortly after Wittgenstein had proved himself in battle during the dreaded Brusilov Offensive)—has him once again complaining about the meanness and nastiness of his fellow soldiers and then blaming himself for being intolerant. It is this remarkable candor that makes Wittgenstein's *Notebooks* so different from the typical war diaries or memoirs of World War I. Most of these, especially the English ones, follow a particular pattern: Herbert Read's *In Retreat*, C. E. Montague's *Disenchantment*, and Siegfried Sassoon's *Memoirs of an Infantry Officer*, for example, detail the horrors of trench warfare in all its misery, placing much of the blame for the war on the British government (often on specific politicians), which put innocent young men into a horrible situation. Often, an idyllic pastoral pre-war England is contrasted to the nightmare of gas masks and barbed wire. When there is relief from horror, it comes in the form of the comradeship brought on by the war, one's new and hitherto unknown fellow soldiers often becoming one's true friends.

Wittgenstein's war diary is the antithesis. He is unlike his English counterparts and unlike such Continental poets as the French Apollinaire, who celebrated *les jeunes de la classe 1915*— young men who appreciated "electrified wires" and, on the eve of war, looked forward to it as a form of revolution:

> Before the war we had only the surface
> Of the earth and the seas
> After it, we'll have the depths
> Subterranean and aerial space[21]

Wittgenstein has nothing to say about the war at all. He neither comments on its politics nor blames Austria-Hungary or Germany for what has happened, nor, except in one brief moment when he speculates that the English will win because they are the "better" people, does he speculate as to which side should or would win. Indeed, the war as a political event holds little interest for him. Rather, he seems to regard *war* as a larger condition—

the existential condition in which one must test oneself. From the first, it is his wish to be sent to the front, to participate in battle so as to determine whether he is brave enough to face death. Later, when he is wounded and decorated, he is deeply relieved that he has passed the bitter test that confronted him. And so, by the time he is made a prisoner of war in Italy in 1918, he has become more serene, more self-confident. And his newly discovered faith in God, or at least in some sort of spiritual reality, has helped him to survive.

At the same time, his attitude toward his fellow men is as negative as the typical war memoirist's is positive. Wittgenstein despises his fellow infantrymen, unable to find the slightest humanity in their boorish and mean-spirited behavior. The officers are different: Some are praised as being very "nice" and "pleasant" people; he spends good evenings conversing with them. But in his assessment of the ordinary military recruits with whom he serves, Wittgenstein betrays all the prejudices of his class. We must remember that he impulsively enlisted as an ordinary soldier when he could easily have been an officer and that the men with whom he served came, not from Vienna or even from Austria, but from the distant Serb, Croat, and Hungarian provinces of the empire. Many were illiterate and did not speak German; no doubt they were a violent, aggressive, and nasty bunch. On the *Goplana*, during his early war months, his fellow recruits evidently made fun of him, taunting and harassing this somewhat delicate, arrogant stranger, who must have appeared, from their perspective, to be a sissy to boot.

In the end, however, the satisfaction of being able to prove himself in battle and to produce the manuscript that was to become the *Tractatus* compensated more than enough for the indignities he had suffered from his peers aboard ship or later at the Eastern

Ludwig Wittgenstein, circa 1908.
Forschungsinstitut Brenner-Archiv
"Familie Wittgenstein-Sammlung
Andreas Sjörgren"
(© *Wittgenstein Initiative*)

Ludwig Wittgenstein, teaching license
photo. c. 1919
(© *Wittgenstein Initiative*)

Front. By 1919 when he returned to Vienna after five long years, Wittgenstein had indeed "become a different person." "The war," he was to remark to a nephew many years later, "saved my life. I don't know what I would have done without it."[22]

—

IN THE DARK SPRING of the 2020 pandemic, I was recovering from back surgery and hence doubly housebound. I turned to Wittgenstein's writings for comfort and enlightenment, and after rereading the *Tractatus* and *Culture and Value*, I found my copy of the *Geheime Tagebücher,* edited by Wilhelm Baum, which I had ordered from Vienna and read shortly after its 1991 publication.* I now reread it with renewed interest but suddenly wondered why I had not seen an English, or at least bilingual, edition of this important text. To my amazement, I found that although many of the choice statements in the *Tagebücher* have been cited by Wittgenstein's biographers, especially Ray Monk, there has never been an English translation of these notebooks. Even the German one is no longer in print because of a copyright controversy, which I discuss in the Afterword.

Surely, I thought, it was time to rectify this omission. My own "special relationship" to Wittgenstein began in the early 1990s, when I discovered those self-declared Wittgensteinian poets and novelists Ingeborg Bachmann and Thomas Bernhard, as well as the Samuel Beckett of the curiously Wittgensteinian novel *Watt*: the result was *Wittgenstein's Ladder*. But my affinity is also something of a family relationship. The inside joke among Viennese Jewish intellectuals of the pre–World War I years was that, given the large families of the *fin de siècle* (Wittgenstein was one of eight children, his father one of eleven), every cultured person was somehow a relative. At the center was Karl Kraus, whose famed weekly paper *Die Fackel* (*The Torch*) Wittgenstein read avidly and frequently cited. The author of the first biographical sketch of Wittgenstein[23] was the famed economist Friedrich von Hayek, who, as it happened, was Wittgenstein's distant cousin. Hayek was also the founder of the so-called *Geistkreis*, an intellectual circle in Vienna to which my father, Maximilian Mintz, belonged. The "family resemblances,"

---

* The title *Geheime Tagebücher* is Wilhelm Baum's, not Wittgenstein's own. The manuscripts in question, reproduced in the *Nachlass* as MS. 101, 102, and 103, have no name; Wittgenstein referred to them simply as his notebooks. "*Geheime*" ("Secret") is somewhat excessive, given that the code used was known to the Wittgenstein siblings. "*Tagebücher*" ("Diaries") is also misleading because Wittgenstein didn't write these notes as a planned diary. So I have chosen to call them *Private Notebooks*, which is more accurate.

which were to become the defining feature of Wittgenstein's "language games," were thus quite real.

The sense of family resemblance also applies to this translation. Like Wittgenstein's, my German is Austrian German—a language different enough from High German to have its own dictionary: one I had used earlier in unpacking some of the curious grammar of Paul Celan for my book *Edge of Irony* and certainly valuable for rendering Wittgenstein's colloquial phrasing.

The translator of the *Private Notebooks*, finally, has to respect Wittgenstein's own silences. "Of what one cannot speak" includes not only the philosophical generalizations and abstractions he so devastatingly deconstructs, but also his private life. Wittgenstein will speak not even to himself about his personal encounters with others. The *Private Notebooks* record no more than "Tonight to the baths" or "My moral standing is now much lower than it was at Easter" or "My relationship with one of the officers—the cadet Adam—is now very tense." The rest is left to the reader's imagination. "If a lion could speak," as Wittgenstein put it in one of his most famous aphorisms, "we would not understand him."

NOTEBOOK 1

August 9, 1914–October 30, 1914

Map of the Austro-Hungarian Empire in 1914,
https://nzhistory.govt.nz/media/photo/map-austro-hungarian-empire-1914
(New Zealand Ministry for Culture and Heritage)

EDITOR'S NOTE

WITTGENSTEIN ENLISTED in the army on August 7, 1914, and was assigned to a regiment on the Eastern Front, near the Polish city of Kraków, then still part of the Austro-Hungarian Empire. Here in western Galicia, the Austrian armies were battling the Russians in a series of futile skirmishes, neither side being able to score a decisive victory.

At first, Wittgenstein was very excited about his new adventure, but, having arrived in Kraków and joined his regiment, he quickly realized he had made a terrible mistake. As someone who could have used his training and connections to become a junior officer but instead enlisted impulsively as an ordinary infantryman, he was to find his options severely limited, and his companions struck him as beings from an alien world. In 1914, class divisions in the empire—and, for that matter, in all of Europe—were still quite rigid, and education was available only to a small percentage of the population.

Wittgenstein's first assignment—as searchlight orderly on the *Goplana*, a patrol ship captured from the Russians on the Vistula

The *Goplana* in Kracòw, with Castle in Background, 1914
(© *Wittgenstein Initiative*)
The *Goplana* on Weichsel River
(© *Wittgenstein Initiative*)

River—was painful. The searchlight had to be looked after at all hours of the night, and his few hours of snatched sleep were on the bare wooden floor of the lower deck with no blankets.

But the night watch was much less taxing than the confrontation with his shipmates. Within a day or two, Wittgenstein was writing in his notebook that his companions were a "pack of rogues" and that he could hardly recognize them as human beings. No doubt the boorish and brawny men, most of them recruited from the distant provinces of Serbia or east-

Goplana, detail, searchlight and cannon machinery
(© Private Collection, Reinhard Mundschütz. Courtesy, Wittgenstein Initiative.)

ern Hungary, made fun of the delicate bookish young man from Vienna, humiliating him at every turn. With no one to love or even converse with, it was a dark time.

A ray of hope came on September 1, when the *Goplana* made a brief stop at the little town of Tarnów, and Wittgenstein, idly exploring a small Polish bookshop on the main square, found a book in German translation that he later claimed saved his life— Tolstoy's *Gospel in Brief* (1892). This revisionary version of the Gospels begins with the premise that "Man is the son of a infinite source, the son of this father not by the flesh, but by the spirit." And, having paid homage to this universal spirit, Tolstoy proceeds to retell the familiar New Testament stories, stripping them of their supernatural component, so that the Agony in the Garden, the Miracle of the Fishes, and so on, become so many moral tales, and Christ no more than an exemplary human being.

Wittgenstein, who had been brought up on the Catholic Catechism (despite his Jewish background), but had never given much thought to religion, pronounced the *Gospel in Brief* "a wonderful book." "But," he added, "I haven't found what I expected in it." What he means, I think, is that although the notion of God as the ineffable spirit within us was very appealing, he wasn't quite satisfied with Tolstoy's rationalizing of the Bible stories. Take the *Gospel in Brief*'s opening:

Tarnow, town square, 1912. On the right is the bookshop (Ksiergarnia) Wittgenstein visited. (© *Wittgenstein Initiative*)

The birth of Jesus Christ happened like this: His mother, Mary, was engaged to Joseph. But before they began to live as husband and wife, it happened that Mary became pregnant. This Joseph was a good man and did not want to disgrace Mary; he took her as his wife and had no relations with her until she gave birth to her first son and named him Jesus.

Wittgenstein, his later comments suggest, preferred the Four Gospels themselves, admiring their language and the mystery and depth of their often enigmatic parables. But for the moment, the protection of *the spirit* helped him to tolerate the insults and taunts of his shipmates. At the same time, Wittgenstein was always a pragmatist. "It is difficult, he writes on September 18, "to serve the spirit on an empty stomach and without sleep."

Boredom, monotony, the constant sound of gunfire, ill-planned movements up and down the tributaries of the Vistula: Despite these conditions, Wittgenstein managed to do quite a bit of his own philosophical work, trying to understand exactly how language could represent reality and to what extent any proposition that is not a tautology could provide certainty. He was, in other words, still writing a treatise on logic.

But the events of war intervened. On September 8, Lemberg (Lvóv or Lviv), the capital of Galicia, was occupied by the Russians, and for the next month, as cold weather began to set in, the *Goplana* was repeatedly docked in riverports close to the battlefront. The nastiness of Wittgenstein's shipmates continued to sting. On September 18, Wittgenstein had overheard "the sergeant badmouthing me to the lieutenant, implying that I had been a coward [on the job]. That upset me terribly." To make matters worse, no letter had yet come from his beloved David Pinsent. "I fought for a

Map of Vistula River Valley

long time against depression," Wittgenstein records on October 12, "then for the first time in ages masturbated." But then on October 20, "my spirit speaks within me countering my depression. May God be with me. —." The Tolstoyan regime seemed to be working.

Then on October 28 the terrible news came that Ludwig's brother, the pianist Paul Wittgenstein, had been wounded in battle and lost his right arm:

Again and again, I have to think of poor Paul, who has
so suddenly been <u>deprived of his vocation</u>! How terrible!
What philosophical outlook would it take to overcome such
a thing? Can it even happen except through suicide!!— I
couldn't work much, but work with assurance. ———. Thy
will be done. ———.

But Paul does not commit suicide. And neither does Ludwig. Note
that, just when circumstances are the worst—and this is typically
the case—Wittgenstein writes that he is doing his philosophical
work "with assurance."

GERMAN TEXT *of* NOTEBOOK 1

ERSTES HEFT, MS. 101

9.8.1914–30.10.1914

Nach meinem Tod zu senden

an Frau

Poldy Wittgenstein

XVII. Neuwalderggerstr. 38

Wien

Zu senden an

Hon. B. Russell

Trinity College

Cambridge

England

ENGLISH TEXT *of* NOTEBOOK 1

FIRST NOTEBOOK, MS. 101

9.8.1914–30.10.1914

After my death to be sent

to Frau

Poldy Wittgenstein

XVII. Neuwalderggerstr. 38

Wien

To be sent to the

Hon. B. Russell

Trinity College

Cambridge

England

9.8.14.

Vorgestern bei der Assentierung genommen worden & dem 2ten Festungs-artillerie-Regiment in Krakau zugeteilt. Gestern vormittag von Wien ab. Komme heute vormittag in Krakau an. Guter Stimmung. Gab mein großes Schreibebuch Trenkler zur Aufbewahrung. Werde ich jetzt arbeiten können??? Sehr gespannt auf mein kommendes Leben! Die Militär-behörden in Wien waren von einer unglaublichen Freundlichkeit. Leute die von Tausenden täglich um Rat gefragt werden gaben freundliche & ausführliche Antworten. So etwas ermutigt ungeheuer. Es erinnerte mich an englische Verhältnisse.

10.8.14.

Als Rekrut eingekleidet worden. Wenig Hoffnung meine technischen Kenntnisse verwenden zu können. Brauch <u>sehr</u> viel gute Laune & Philosophie um mich hier zurecht zu finden. Als ich heute aufwachte war es mir wie in einem jener Träume worin man plötzlich ganz unsinniger Weise wieder in der Schule sitzt. In meiner Stellung ist freilich auch viel Humor & ich verrichte die niedrigsten Dienste mit fast ironischem Lächeln. Nicht gearbeitet. Dies ist eine Feuerprobe des Charakters eben darum weil so viel Kraft dazu gehört die gute Stimmung & die Energie nicht zu verlieren.

9.8.14.

The day before yesterday I enlisted as a volunteer & was assigned to the 2nd Garrison Artillery Regiment in Kraków. Off from Vienna yesterday morning. I arrived this morning in Kraków. Good mood. Gave my large notebook to Trenkler* for safekeeping. Will I be able to work now???** Very curious about my future life! The military authorities in Vienna were unbelievably friendly. Officials who are asked for help by thousands every day gave gracious & detailed replies. This kind of thing is enormously encouraging. It reminded me of the English way of doing things.

10.8.14.

Put on my recruit uniform. Little hope of being able to use my technical skills.*** I'll need a <u>great deal</u> of good humor and philosophy to feel at home here. When I woke up this morning, I felt as if I were in the middle of one of those dreams in which, for no reason at all, you are suddenly sitting in a schoolroom. Given my position, there is of course much to laugh at & I perform the most menial tasks, smiling ironically. I have done none of my own work. The situation here is a test of fire of one's character, precisely because it takes so much strength not to lose one's temper & one's energy.

---

* Adolf Trenkler, Wittgenstein family secretary. The notebook in question contains pre-war entries on logic, some handwritten, some typed. Wittgenstein's sister Hermine ("Mining") mentions receiving the "large ledger" in a letter to him of June 7, 1917; see McGuinness, *Wittgenstein's Family Letters*, 28–29.

** "Work" always refers to Wittgenstein's personal work on his ongoing treatise on the rules of logic that he had begun writing during his stay in Norway in 1913.

*** The reference is to Wittgenstein's training in mechanical engineering at the Technische Hochschule at Charlottenburg in Berlin (1906–1908), followed by informal research in aeronautics at the University of Manchester until 1911, when he moved to Cambridge to study logic and philosophy with Bertrand Russell.

11.8.14.

Schlecht geschlafen (Ungeziefer). Nachdem ich das Zimmer gekehrt hatte marschierten wir zu ein paar alten Mörsern & wurden im Gebrauch instruiert. Furchtbar heiß. Das Essen ist uneßbar. Werde vielleicht in Zukunft außerhalb der Kaserne schlafen. An David geschrieben. Sehne mich schon nach einem Brief von ihm um das Gefühl des Kontakts mit meinem früheren Leben nicht zu verlieren. Noch nicht gearbeitet.

13.8.14.

Vorgestern beim Hauptmann gewesen. War sehr verdattert & stand nicht militärmäßig vor ihm. Er war etwas ironisch und mir nicht recht sympathisch. Resultat = 0. Heute kam es heraus daß ich Matura etc. gemacht hatte worauf eine ganze Reihe der Einjährigen mich mit Herr Kollege betitelten & auf mich eindrangen ich solle doch mein Freiwilligenrecht geltend machen. Dies machte mir Spaß. (It bucked me up.) Gestern & heute starken Katarrh & oft Unwohlbefinden. Manchmal ein wenig deprimiert. Traf heute in der Kantine einen Leutnant dem es auffiel daß ich dort zu Mittag aß. Er fragte mich sehr nett was ich im Zivil sei wunderte sich sehr daß sie mich nicht zu den einjährig Freiwilligen genommen hatten & war überhaupt sehr freundlich was mir sehr wohl tat.

11.8.14.

Slept badly (bedbugs). After I swept the room, we marched over to a couple of old mortars and were taught how to use them. Terribly hot. The food is inedible. Perhaps in the future I will sleep outside the barracks. Wrote to David.[1] Already longing for a letter from him so as not to lose the feeling of contact with my previous life. Done no work yet.

13.8.14.

Day before yesterday at the captain's. I was quite rattled & didn't appear appropriately military to him. He was a little sarcastic toward me and I didn't find him very likeable. Result = 0. Today it emerged that I had taken the Matura* etc., whereupon a whole bunch of *Einjährigen*** started calling me *Herr Kollege* and insisted that I should claim my rights as a volunteer. That gave me a lift. (*It bucked me up.*)*** Yesterday and today a bad cough & I was often feeling unwell. Sometimes a little depressed. Today in the canteen I met a lieutenant who noticed I was taking my dinner there. He asked very nicely what my occupation was in civil life, wondered why they hadn't put me with the *Einjähriger* volunteers, & was altogether very friendly, which did me a lot of good.

---

* Secondary school exit exam, rather like the baccalaureate degree ("Bac") in France and roughly comparable to the *A-levels* in the United Kingdom.

** The term *Einjährigen* refers to the Austrian army's *Einjährig-Freiwillig* status, the one-year volunteer service, open to enlisted soldiers who had passed the *Matura* and signed on for conscription at their own cost in exchange for the opportunity for promotion to reserve officer status.

*** The parenthetical remark is in English in the original.

15.8.14.

Es geschieht so viel daß mir ein Tag so lange vorkommt wie eine Woche. Bin gestern zur Bedienung eines Scheinwerfers auf einem von uns gekaperten Schiffe auf der Weichsel beordert worden. Die Bemannung ist eine Saubande! Keine Begeisterung, unglaubliche Rohheit, Dummheit & Bosheit! Es ist also doch nicht wahr daß die gemeinsame große Sache die Menschen adeln <u>muß</u>. Hierdurch wird auch die lästigste Arbeit zum Frondienst. Es ist merkwürdig wie sich die Menschen ihre Arbeit selbst zu einer häßlichen Mühsal machen. Unter allen unseren äußeren Umständen könnte die Arbeit auf diesem Schiffe eine herrliche glückliche Zeit geben und statt dessen!—Es wird wohl unmöglich sein sich hier mit den Leuten zu verständigen (außer etwa mit dem Leutnant der ein ganz netter Mensch zu sein scheint). Also in <u>Demut</u> die Arbeit verrichten und sich selbst um Gottes willen nicht verlieren!!!! Nämlich am leichtesten verliert man sich selbst wenn man sich anderen Leuten schenken will.

16.8.14.

Auf der "Goplana". Nochmals: Die Dummheit, Frechheit & Bosheit dieser Menschen kennt keine Grenzen. Jede Arbeit wird zur Qual. Aber ich habe heute schon wieder gearbeitet & werde mich nicht unterkriegen lassen. Schrieb heute eine Karte an den lieben David. Der Himmel beschütze ihn & erhalte mir seine Freundschaft!— Die Fahrt selbst entlang der Weichsel ist herrlich & ich bin in guter Stimmung.

17.8.14.

Ein Gaunerpack! Die Offiziere nur sind nette Menschen & zum Teil wirklich <u>sehr</u> fein. Müssen auf der bloßen Erde schlafen & ohne Decken. Sind jetzt in Rußland. Durch die schwere Arbeit bin ich ganz unsinnig geworden. Heute noch nicht gearbeitet. Auf dem

15.8.14.

So much is happening that a day feels as long as a week. Yesterday I was assigned the post of searchlight orderly on one of the gunboats captured by us on the Vistula; my shipmates are a bunch of swine! No enthusiasm for anything, unbelievable crudity, stupidity & malice! So it turns out not to be true that a great common cause <u>inevitably</u> ennobles people. As it is, even the most trivial jobs become a chore. It is remarkable how people turn work itself into ugly hardship. Given all our external circumstances, working on this ship could be a wonderfully happy time and instead!—It will probably be impossible to have any sort of understanding with these men (except perhaps with the Lieutenant, who seems to be quite a nice person). So, no choice but to carry out one's work in all <u>humility</u> and for God's sake not to lose oneself!!!! For the easiest way to lose oneself is to want to give oneself to other people.

16.8.14.

Aboard the "Goplana." Again: the stupidity, insolence and malice of this bunch knows no limits. Every job turns into torture. But today I did my own work again & will not let myself get discouraged. Also, wrote a card to dear David. May heaven protect him and maintain our friendship!—The trip itself down the Vistula is beautiful and I am in a good mood.

17.8.14.

A pack of rogues! Only the officers are nice people & in part really <u>very</u> refined. We have to sleep on the bare ground and without blankets. We are now in Russia! Because of the hard labor I've become quite asexual. Today have not yet done my own work. God be with

Deck ist es zu kalt & unten sind zu viel Menschen die sprechen, schreien, stinken etc. etc.

18.8.14.
Nachts um 1 werde ich plötzlich geweckt, der Oberleutnant fragt nach mir & sagt ich müsse sofort zum Scheinwerfer. "Nicht anziehen". Ich lief fast nackt auf die Kommandobrücke. Eisige Luft, Regen. Ich war sicher jetzt würde ich sterben. Setzte den Scheinwerfer in Gang & zurück mich anzukleiden. Es war falscher Alarm. Ich war <u>furchtbar</u> aufgeregt & stöhnte laut. Ich empfand die Schrecken des Krieges. Jetzt (abends) habe ich den Schreck schon wieder überwunden. Ich werde mein Leben mit aller Kraft zu erhalten trachten wenn ich nicht meinen gegenwärtigen Sinn ändere.

21.8.14.
Der Leutnant & ich haben schon oft über alles Mögliche gesprochen; ein sehr netter Mensch. Er kann mit den größten Halunken umgehen & freundlich sein ohne sich etwas zu vergeben. Wenn wir einen Chinesen hören so sind wir geneigt sein Sprechen für ein unartikuliertes Gurgeln zu halten. Einer der Chinesisch versteht wird darin die Sprache erkennen. So kann ich oft nicht den Menschen im Menschen erkennen etc. Ein wenig aber erfolglos gearbeitet. Ob es jetzt für immer mit meinem Arbeiten aus ist?!!! Das weiß der Teufel. Ob mir nie mehr etwas einfallen wird? Ich bin mit allen den Begriffen meiner Arbeit ganz & gar "unfamiliär." Ich <u>sehe</u> gar nichts!!!!

22.8.14.
Stehen schon 3 Tage auf einer Sandbank. Arbeite oft mit vielen Unterbrechungen und bisher ganz erfolglos. Kann noch immer auf nichts <u>Festes</u> kommen. Alles geht in Dunst auf. Nur zu!!!

me. On deck it is too cold & below there are too many men who talk, scream, stink, etc. etc.

18.8.14.

At night at 1 o'clock I am suddenly awakened, the first lieutenant is asking for me & says I must come up immediately to operate the searchlight. "Don't get dressed." I ran practically naked to the navigating bridge. Icy air, rain. I was sure that now I would die. Turned on the searchlight & dashed back to get dressed. It was a false alarm. I was <u>terribly</u> agitated & groaned out loud. I felt the horrors of war. Now (evening) I've gotten over the horror. Unless I change my mind, I will strive with all my might to stay alive.

21.8.14.

The Lieutenant & I have already spoken frequently about all sorts of things; a very nice person. He knows how to handle the worst rascals & be pleasant without losing his self-possession. When we hear a Chinese man talking, we are inclined to take his speech as so much inarticulate gurgling. But someone who knows Chinese will be able to recognize the language inside the sound. Just so, I often cannot recognize the *human being* inside the human being. Worked a little bit but without success. Or is it now over with my work forever?!!! The devil knows. Will no idea ever enter my mind again? With all the concepts central to my work, I now feel completely "unfamiliar." I <u>see</u> nothing at all!!!

22.8.14.

For 3 days already we have been stuck on a sandbank. I often work on the logic material with many interruptions and until now quite unsuccessfully. Still can't come up with anything <u>solid</u>. Everything goes up in smoke. Go ahead and do it!!!

25.8.14.

Gestern ein furchtbarer Tag. Abends wollte der Scheinwerfer nicht funktionieren. Als ich ihn untersuchen wollte wurde ich von der Mannschaft durch Zurufe, Grölen etc. gestört. Wollte ihn genauer untersuchen, da nahm ihn der Zugsführer mir aus der Hand. Ich kann gar nicht weiter schreiben. Es war entsetzlich. Das Eine habe ich gesehen: Es ist nicht ein einziger anständiger Kerl in der ganzen Mannschaft. Wie aber soll ich mich in Zukunft zu dem Allen stellen? Soll ich einfach dulden? Und wenn ich das nicht tun will? Dann muß ich in einem fortwährenden Kampf leben. Was ist besser? Im 2. Fall würde ich mich <u>sicher</u> aufreiben. Im ersten <u>vielleicht</u> nicht. Es wird jetzt für mich eine <u>enorm</u> schwere Zeit kommen denn ich bin jetzt tatsächlich wieder so verkauft & verraten wie seinerzeit in der Schule in Linz. Nur eines ist nötig: Alles was einem geschieht betrachten können; <u>sich sammeln</u>! Gott helfe mir!

26.8.14.

Habe mir gestern vorgenommen <u>keinen Widerstand zu leisten</u>. Mein Äußeres so zu sagen ganz leicht zu machen um mein Inneres ungestört zu lassen.

29.8.14.

Jede Nacht stehe ich auf der Kommandobrücke bis etwa 3½ a.m. Mein Vorhaben der vollkommenen Passivität habe ich noch nicht recht ausgeführt. Die Niedertracht der Kameraden ist mir noch immer schrecklich. Aber nur bei sich bleiben! Arbeite täglich etwas aber noch ohne rechten Erfolg. Obwohl schon manches aufdämmert.

25.8.14.

Yesterday a terrible day. In the evening the searchlight would not function. As I was trying to fix it, I was interrupted by my shipmates with shouts and catcalls etc. I was trying to examine it more thoroughly when the sergeant in charge grabbed it from my hand. I can hardly continue to write. It was horrible. There's one thing I've learned: there is not a single decent fellow in the whole crew. But how should I conduct myself in response to all this in the future? Shall I simply endure it? And if I don't wish to do that? Then I must undergo a constant struggle. Which is better? In the second case, I would <u>surely</u> wear myself out. In the first, <u>maybe</u> not. It will now be an <u>enormously</u> difficult time for me because I have literally been sold & betrayed again just as I was years ago when I was at school in Linz.* Only one thing is necessary: to maintain one's distance from everything that happens; to <u>collect oneself</u>! God help me!

26.8.14.

I resolved yesterday to <u>mount no opposition</u>. To lighten up, so to speak, my outer self, so as to allow my inner being to be undisturbed.

29.8.14.

Every night I stand watch on the navigation bridge till around 3:30 a.m. I have not quite managed to carry out my resolution to practice complete passivity. The mendacity of these "comrades" is still awful for me to bear. One must just be true to oneself! Work every day a little but not with any tangible success. Although a little light is beginning to dawn.

---

* Wittgenstein was tutored at home until he was fourteen; in 1903 he was sent to the *k.u.k. Realschule* in Linz, receiving a more technical, less classical education than he would have received at a gymnasium. According to all acounts, Wittgenstein always felt he did not fit in, referring, in his journal, to "suffering in class" and lack of rapport with his classmates.

2.9.14.

Jede Nacht mit Ausnahme von gestern beim Scheinwerfer. Am Tag schlafe ich. Dieser Dienst ist mir in so fern angenehm als ich dadurch der Bosheit der Kameraden mehr entzogen bin. Gestern hörten wir hier von einer enormen Schlacht die schon 5 Tage im Gang sei. Wäre es nur schon die Entscheidung! Gestern zum ersten Mal seit 3 Wochen onaniert. Bin fast ganz unsinnlich. Während ich mir früher immer Gespräche mit einem Freund vorstellte geschieht dies jetzt fast nie. Arbeite täglich ein ganz klein wenig bin aber zu müde und abgelenkt. Gestern fing ich an in Tolstois Erläuterungen zu den Evangelien zu lesen. Ein herrliches Werk. Es ist mir aber noch nicht das was ich davon erwartete.

4.9.14.

Es geht!—Nur Mut! — Arbeite viel.

5.9.14.

Ich bin auf dem Wege zu einer großen Entdeckung. Aber ob ich dahingelangen werde?! Bin sinnlicher als früher. Heute wieder onaniert. Draußen ist es eisig & stürmisch. Ich liege auf dem Stroh am Boden & schreibe & lese auf einem kleinen Holzkoffer (Preis 2'50 Kronen).

2.9.14.

Every night except the last I've been operating the searchlight. During the day I sleep. This schedule is agreeable to me insofar as it removes me further from the malice of my comrades. Yesterday we heard of an enormous battle already in progress for 5 days.* If only it were already over! Yesterday for the first time in 3 weeks, masturbated. I am almost entirely free of sexual desire. Whereas earlier I always imagined conversations with a friend, this almost never happens now. I work a little bit every day but am too tired and distracted. Yesterday I began to read Tolstoy's *Gospel in Brief.*** A wonderful book. But I haven't yet found what I expected from it.

4.9.14.

Things are alright!—Courage! — Working hard.

5.9.14.

I am on the way to a great discovery. But will I manage to get there? Feeling more erotic than before. Masturbated again today. It is freezing and stormy outside. I am lying on some straw on the floor and writing and reading on a little wooden suitcase (Price 2.50 crowns).

---

* The reference is to the battle with the Russian forces at Kraśnik, the first in a series of battles that forced the *Goplana* to head back to Kraków.

** By chance, in a small bookshop in Tarnów (see the photo on p. 24), where the *Goplana* made a brief stop, Wittgenstein found and purchased a copy of Tolstoy's *Gospel in Brief,* which became a bible to him in the coming war days. Tolstoy's *Gospel,* an amalgam of the Four Gospels of the New Testament, with an emphasis on John, eliminates the New Testament references to the afterlife and characterizes the miracles as merely metaphoric, focusing on the human Jesus, who teaches us that man must renounce the flesh and free himself from all petty practical concerns, living only for the spirit.

6.9.14.
Werde von den meisten Kameraden nach wie vor gequält. Ich habe noch immer kein Verhalten dagegen gefunden das zufriedenstellend wäre. Zur volkommenen Passivität habe ich mich noch nicht entschlossen. Und wahrscheinlich ist das eine Torheit; denn ich bin ja gegen alle diese Menschen ohnmächtig. Ich reibe mich <u>nutzlos</u> auf wenn ich mich wehre.

8.9.14.
Erfuhr heute früh daß Lemberg von den Russen besetzt sei. Jetzt weiß ich daß wir hin sind! In den letzen 4 Tagen nicht Nachtdiest gehabt weil sehr helle Nächte waren. Jeden Tag viel garbeitet & viel in Tolstoï's Erläuterung gelesen.

10.9.14.
Viel zu tun. Trotzem ziemlich gearbeitet. Ohne bestimmten Erfolg aber nicht in der gewissen hoffnunglosen Stimmung.

12.9.14.
Die Nachrichten werden immer schlechter. Heute nacht wird strenge Bereitschaft sein. Ich arbeite täglich mehr oder weniger und recht zuversichtlich. Immer wieder sage ich mir im Geiste die Worte Tolstois vor: "Der Mensch ist <u>ohnmächtig</u> im Fleische aber <u>frei</u> durch den Geist." Möge der Geist in mir sein! Nachmittag hörte der Leutnant Schüsse in der Nähe. Ich wurde sehr aufgeregt. Wahrscheinlich werden wir alarmiert werden. Wie werde ich mich benehmen wenn es zum Schießen kommt? Ich fürchte mich nicht davor erschossen zu werden aber davor meine Pflicht nicht ordentlich zu erfüllen. Gott gebe mir Kraft! Amen. Amen. Amen.

6.9.14.

Being tortured by most of my shipmates, now as before. I still haven't found the proper mode of behavior that would be satisfactory. I have not yet opted for complete passivity. And perhaps this is folly; since I am powerless against all these fellows. I overexcite myself for <u>nothing</u> if I resist.

8.9.14.

I learned this morning that Lemberg* has been occupied by the Russians. Now I know we're done for! For the last 4 days I've had no night duty because we have had white nights. Every day have worked hard and read a great deal in Tolstoy's *Gospel*.

10.9.14.

Much to do. Nevertheless worked pretty hard. Without appreciable success but not in that certain hopeless mood.

12.9.14.

The news gets worse all the time. Tonight there will be strict active duty orders. I work every day, more or less, and with some confidence. Over and over again I say to myself the words of Tolstoy, "Man is <u>helpless</u> in the flesh but <u>free</u> in the spirit." May the spirit be within me! In the afternoon the lieutenant heard shots in the vicinity. I became very anxious. Probably we will be attacked. How will I behave when it comes to being shot at? I am afraid, not of being killed but of not fulfilling my duty properly before that moment. God give me strength. Amen. Amen. Amen.

---

* Lemberg (*Lvóv* in Polish, *Lviv* in Ukrainian) was an ancient city and cultural center that became the capital of Galicia, the large eastern province of the former Austro-Hungarian Empire (see the map on p. 20). After World War I, it was deeded to Poland; after World War II, it belonged first to the Soviet Union and in 1991 became part of the newly independent Ukraine.

13.9.14.
Heute in aller Früh verließen wir das Schiff mit allem was darauf war. Die Russen sind uns auf den Fersen. Habe furchtbare Szenen miterlebt. Seit 30 Stunden nicht geschlafen; fühle mich sehr schwach und sehe keine äußere Hoffnung. Wenn es mit mir jetzt zu Ende geht so möge ich einen guten Tod sterben, eingedenk meiner selbst. Möge ich mich nie selbst verlieren.

15.9.14.
Vorgestern nachts furchtbare Szenen: fast alle Leute besoffen. Gestern wieder auf die Goplana zurück die in den Dunajec gefahren wurde. Gestern & vorgestern nicht gearbeitet. Versuchte vergeblich, meinem Kopf war die ganz Sache fremd. Die Russen sind uns auf den Fersen. Wir sind in unmittelbarer Nähe des Feindes. Bin guter Stimmung, habe wieder gearbeitet. Am besten kann ich jetzt arbeiten während ich Kartoffeln schäle. Melde mich immer freiwillig dazu. Es ist für mich dasselbe was das Linsenschleifen für Spinoza war. Mit dem Leutnant stehe ich viel kühler als früher. Aber nur Mut!

"Wen der Genius nicht verläßt – – – –"! Gott mit mir! Jetzt wäre mir Gelegenheit gegeben ein anständiger Mensch zu sein denn ich stehe vor dem Tod Aug in Auge. Möge der Geist mich erleuchten.

16.9.14.
Die Nacht verging ruhig. Vormittag starkes Geschützfeuer & Gewehrfeuer gehört. Wir sind aller Wahrscheinlichkeit nach unentrinnbar verloren. Der Geist ist noch bei mir aber ob er mich nicht in der äußersten Not verlassen wird? Ich hoffe nicht! Jetzt sich nur zusammennehmen und brav sein! (9 p.m.) Wolkenbruch. Der

13.9.14.

At dawn this morning, we abandoned the ship with everything on it. The Russians are at our heels. I have experienced some terrible scenes. I have not slept for 30 hours; feel very weak and see no reason for hope. If this is the end for me, may I die a good death, worthy of my best self. May I never lose my self.

15.9.14.

Night before last, terrible scenes: practically everyone drunk. Yesterday back on the Goplana, which had been sailed down the Dunajec. No work, yesterday and day before yesterday. Tried in vain, the whole thing was alien to my mind. The Russians are at our heels. We are in immediate proximity of the enemy. I'm in a good mood, worked again. I can think best right now when I am peeling potatoes. Always volunteer for it. It is for me what grinding lenses was for Spinoza.* My relationship with the lieutenant is much cooler than before. But give me courage!

"He whom his genius does not desert − − − −"** God be with me! Now would be my chance to become a decent human being since I am face-to-face with death. May the spirit enlighten me.

16.9.14.

The night passed quietly. In the morning heard heavy cannonade & rifle fire. We are, in all probability, inescapably lost. The spirit is still with me but will it abandon me in my most utmost need? I hope not! Now one can only collect oneself and be brave (9 p.m.).

---

* Wittgenstein first encountered the great Dutch seventeenth-century moral philosopher Spinoza at his high school in Linz and became a great admirer. In his day job, Spinoza worked as an optical lens grinder.
** Here Wittgenstein cites the first line of Goethe's famous "Wandrer's Sturmlied," "Wem du nicht verlässest, Genius," a prayer begging the spirit of nature not to desert the poet.

Mensch ist ohnmächtig im Fleische und <u>frei durch den Geist</u>. Und nur durch diesen. Fast nichts gearbeitet.

17.9.14.

Auch diese Nacht ruhig vorüber gegangen. Hatte Wache. Wir sollen die Weichsel hinauf nach Krakau fahren. Die Grenze soll ganz von Kosaken besetzt sein also sind wir wahrscheinlich hin. Nur <u>eines</u> ist von Nöten! Gestern früh hat der Leutnant das Schiff verlassen und ist bis heute mittag noch nicht zurückgekommen. Niemand weiß was wir tun sollen und es mangelt sogar an Geld zum Einkaufen von Essen: Ich bin aber noch immer guter Dinge und werde es hoffentlich bleiben. Denke immer wieder daran wie ich mich aufrecht erhalten kann.

18.9.14.

Eine furchtbar aufregende Nacht. Sollte leuchten und mußte jeden Moment befürchten daß der Scheinwerfer ausgeht. Wir waren in einer höchst unsicheren Stellung und wäre das Licht ausgegangen & etwas geschehen so wäre die ganze Verantwortung auf mich gefallen. Dann falscher Alarm; ich behielt vollkommene Ruhe & mußte hören wie mich der Zugsführer beim Leutnant schlecht zu machen suchte, als sei ich furchtsam gewesen. Dies regte mich furchtbar auf. Von 1–3 auf Posten. Sehr wenig geschlafen. Gestern nicht gearbeitet. Es ist unendlich schwer sich dem Bösen nicht zu widersetzen. Es ist schwer mit leerem Magen und unausgeschlafen dem Geiste zu dienen. Aber was wäre ich wenn ich es nicht könnte. Die Vorgesetzten sind grob & dumm, die Kameraden sind dumm & grob (mit ganz wenigen Ausnahmen.) Auf der Fahrt nach Krakau mit Galeeren. Der Tag verlief ruhig und nicht unangenehm. Etwas gearbeitet. —

Downpour. Man is powerless in the flesh and <u>free in the spirit</u>. And only through the spirit. Did almost no work.

17.9.14.

This night passed quietly too. I was on watch. We are supposed to be going up the Vistula toward Kraków. The border is evidently occupied by Cossacks so we are probably done for. Only <u>one thing</u> is notable! Yesterday morning the lieutenant left the ship and had not returned by noon today. Nobody knows what we are supposed to be doing and there isn't even enough money to buy food: but I am still in a good frame of mind and hope to stay that way. I am always thinking of how I can keep myself upright.

18.9.14.

A terribly upsetting night. I was supposed to provide light and was afraid every minute that the searchlight would go out. We were in a very unsafe situation, and if the light had gone out and something had happened, the whole responsibility would have been mine. Then false alarm; I didn't make a sound & had to hear the sergeant badmouthing me to the lieutenant, implying that I had been a coward. That upset me terribly. From 1–3 was at the post. Slept very little. Yesterday did no work. It is infinitely hard not to resist evil. It is difficult to serve the spirit on an empty stomach and without sleep. But what would I be if I could not do it? The regulations are crude & stupid, the men (with very few exceptions) are stupid & crude. On the way to Kraków with galleys. The day passed quietly and was not unpleasant. Worked a bit. —

19.9.14.

Nach Krakau. Gestern abends mußte ich auf einem anderen Schiff bei der Arbeit bis 11 Uhr leuchten. In der Nacht sehr kalt. Wir mußten in Stiefeln schlafen. Schlecht geschlafen. Schon seit 4 Tagen habe ich meine Kleider & Schuhe nicht ausgezogen. Aber das darf nichts machen. — Ich kann nicht umhin mich davor zu fürchten was mit mir in Krakau geschehen wird. Ich weiß ich sollte mir darüber keine Sorge machen, aber ich fühle mich so müde daß ich mich vor jeder Anstrengung fürchte. —!

20.9.14.

Ja, nochmals: Es ist unendlich <u>schwer</u> sich der Bosheit der Menschen nicht zu widersetzen! Denn die Bosheit der Menschen schlägt einem jedes Mal eine Wunde. — Die Russen sind von der Grenze soweit vertrieben worden daß wir bis jetzt noch nicht belästigt worden sind.

21.9.14.

Heute früh in Krakau angekommen. Die ganze Nacht beim Reflektor Dienst gehabt. Gestern viel gearbeitet aber nicht <u>sehr</u> hoffnungsvoll da mir der rechte <u>Überblick</u> fehlte. Hatte gestern eine kleine Aussprache mit unserem Zugsführer die die Luft ein <u>wenig</u> reinigte. Heute etwas mißgestimmt: Ich bin die vielen Aufregungen schon so <u>müde</u>! Von Wien höre ich gar nichts! Heute erhielt ich eine Karte von Mama die sie am 20.8. schrieb. Abends erhielt ich die niederschlagende Nachricht daß der Leutnant der unser Kommandant war transferiert worden ist. Diese Nachricht hat mich tief deprimiert. Ich kann mir zwar keine genaue Rechenschaft ablegen über eine zwingende Ursache zur Niedergeschlagenheit aber ich bin tief traurig. Ich bin zwar frei durch den Geist aber der Geist hat mich verlassen! Konnte am Abend noch etwas arbeiten, fühlte mich darauf besser. —.

19.9.14.

To Kraków. Last night I had to work on another ship, operating the searchlight till 11 o'clock. At night, very cold. We had to sleep with our boots on. I slept badly. I have not taken off my clothes & shoes for four days. But that doesn't matter. — I cannot stop fearing what will happen to me in Kraków. I know I should not upset myself about it, but I feel so tired that I am afraid of any exertion. —!

20.9.14.

Yes, again: it is infinitely <u>hard</u> not to take a stand against the malice of human beings! For the malice of human beings inflicts a wound every time. — The Russians have been driven so far back from the border that at least until now, we have not been bothered by them.

21.9.14.

Arrived in Kraków this morning. I was on searchlight duty all night. Yesterday worked a great deal but not <u>very</u> hopeful because I am missing the right <u>overview</u>. Yesterday I had a little private talk with our sergeant which cleared the air <u>a bit</u>. Today I am slightly out of sorts: I'm already so <u>exhausted</u> from the endless excitement. I hear nothing at all from Vienna! Today I received a card from Mama which she wrote on 20.8. In the evening I received the crushing news that the lieutenant who was our commander has been transferred. This news deeply depressed me. I can't really give an exact account of the immediate cause of my depression but I am profoundly sad. I am of course free in the spirit but now the spirit has left me! In the evening I worked a little, therefore felt a little better. —.

22.9.14.

Vormittag in der Kaserne um Geld zu holen, beim Hauptmann. Er sagte ich solle mir die Einjährigen-Streifen aufnähen lassen. Viele Besorgungen gemacht und auf's Schiff zurück wo die Streifen großes Aufsehen erregten. Erhielt eine Menge Karten & Briefe u.a. von Ficker & Jolles. Nicht gearbeitet. —.

23.9.14.

Etwas gearbeitet.

24.9.14.

Ziemlich viel gearbeitet aber ziemlich hoffnungslos. Nachmittags in der Stadt.

25.9.14.

Ziemlich viel gearbeitet aber ohne echte Zuversicht. Es fehlt mir noch immer der Überblick und dadurch erscheint das Problem unübersehbar.

27.9.14.

Gestern ziemlich gearbeitet aber ohne rechten Erfolg. In den letzten Tagen wieder etwas sinnlich. Telegrafierte gestern nach Hause und bat um Nachricht.

22.9.14.

To the barracks in the morning to get money, see the captain. He said I should have the Einjährigen stripes sewn on. I made many purchases and came back aboard where the stripes made a great impression. Received many cards & letters incl. from Ficker* & Jolles.** Did no work. —.

23.9.14.

Did some work.

24.9.14.

Worked pretty hard but without much hope. Afternoon in town.

25.9.14.

Worked pretty hard but without real confidence. I am still lacking an overview and accordingly the problem seems incalculable.

27.9.14.

Yesterday worked quite a bit but without real results. In the last few days once again some sexual desire. Yesterday telegraphed home and begged for some news.

---

* Ludwig von Ficker (1880–1967), the editor of the literary journal *Der Brenner*, based in Innsbruck. Shortly before the war in 1914, Wittgenstein offered Ficker the princely sum of 100,000 Kronen (c. $150,000 today) to distribute among needy poets and artists of Ficker's choice: Among them were Georg Trakl, Rainer Marie Rilke, and Adolf Loos. Wittgenstein knew little about contemporary poets or artists and made this offer more or less on impulse, having read about Ficker's journal in Karl Kraus's *Die Fackel* and having recently inherited his share of the large fortune of his father, Karl, who died in January 1913.

** Adele Jolles, the wife of Stanislaus Jolles (1857–1942), who was Wittgenstein's teacher and mentor at the Technische Hochschule at Charlottenburg in Berlin between 1906 and 1908. L.W. boarded with the Jolles family in this period, and Adele took a great interest in him and later wrote him regularly.

28.9.14.

Etwas gearbeitet. Man erwartet eine Belagerung von Krakau. Wenn sie eintritt so stehen uns noch schwere Zeiten bevor. Möge der Geist mir Kraft schenken!

29.9.14.

Heute morgen einen Korporal in's Spital gebracht der an Ruhr erkrankt ist. Hier kommen jetz viel Ruhrfälle vor. Es wird mir eigentümlich zumute, wenn ich denke, was ich in diesem Kriege noch alles erleben müssen werde. Gearbeitet aber ohne Erfolg. Ich sehe noch immer nicht klar und habe keinen Überblick. Ich sehe Einzelheiten ohne zu wissen wie sie sich in das Ganze einfügen werden. Darum auch fühle ich jedes neue Problem als eine Bürde. Während ein klarer Überblick zeigen müßte daß jedes Problem das Hauptproblem ist und der Anblick der Hauptfragen ermattet nicht sondern er stärkt! Abends nicht ohne Erfolg gearbeitet. Nur Mut!—

30.9.14

Heute Nacht begann ich mich unwohl zu fühlen. (Magen & Kopf). Dein Wille geschehe!

1.10.14

Gestern mußte ich mich am Vormittag hinlegen und den ganze Tag liegenbleiben da ich mich sehr unwohl fühlte. Ziemlich viel gearbeitet, aber ohne Erfolg. Es heißt daß wir morgen von diesem Schiff weg sollen. Ich bin neugierig was mit mir geschehen wird. —!

28.9.14.

Worked a bit. We're awaiting an attack from Kraków. If it happens we will be facing hard times. May the spirit grant me power!

29.9.14.

A corporal who has contracted dysentery was taken to the hospital this morning. There are now many cases of dysentery here. It gives me a strange feeling to think of everything I must still live through in the course of this war. Worked but without success. I still don't see clearly and have no overview. I see details without knowing what role they will play in the whole. For this reason, I also perceive every new problem as a burden. Whereas a clear overview would have to show that each problem is the problem and that a consideration of the main questions does not exhaust the case but rather strengthens it! In the evening worked but not without success. Courage!——

30.9.14.

Tonight began to feel sick. (stomach & head). Thy will be done!

1.10.14.

Yesterday I had to lie down in the morning and stay in bed all day since I felt very ill. I worked quite a bit but without success. The word is that tomorrow we are supposed to leave this ship. I am curious to know what is to become of me. ——!

2.10.14.

Ziemlich viel gearbeitet. Nicht ganz ohne Erfolg. Es ist noch immer unbestimmt was mit mir geschehen wird, ob ich auf dem Schiff bleibe oder nicht etc. etc.

3.10.14.

Es ist heute die Bestimmung getroffen worden daß die ganze alte Mannschaft dieses Schiffes, mit Ausnahme von 4 Mann darunter ich, das Schiff verlassen soll. Dies ist mir nicht unangenehm. Von Zuhause erhielt ich heute eine Kiste worin warme Wäsche, Tee, Zwieback & Schokolade war. Also gerade als ob die liebe Mama sie geschickt hätte; aber keine Nachricht! Ist Mama tot? Und schickt man mir darum keine Nachricht?? Fast nicht gearbeitet.

4.10.14.

Gestern abends noch etwas gearbeitet. Erhielt heute eine Karte die Mama an mich am 9. des vorigen Monats geschrieben hat. Sie enthält nichts Wichtiges. Meine Arbeit ist nach kurzem Aufschwung heute wieder ins Stocken geraten. Ziemlich viel gearbeitet aber ohne Hoffnung. In den nächsten Tagen sollen wir wieder nach Rußland fahren. Unser neuer Kommandant, ein Oberleutnant, gefällt mir nicht recht obwohl ich ihn nur flüchtig gesehen habe.

5.10.14.

Heute erhielt ich einen Brief von Keynes der über Norwegen an's hiesige Regimentskommando kam! Er schreibt nur um mich zu fragen

2.10.14.

Worked quite a lot. Not without some success. It has still not been decided what is to become of me, whether I am to stay on the ship or not etc. etc.

3.10.14.

Today the decision was reached that the entire crew of this ship, with the exception of 4 men, <u>myself</u> included, will leave the ship. This is not unpleasant to me. From home, I received a crate containing warm underwear, tea, Zwiebach & chocolate. So it's just as if dear Mama had sent it herself; <u>but</u> <u>no</u> <u>news</u>! Is Mama dead? And is that why they are not sending me any news??? I did almost no work.

4.10.14.

Yesterday evening managed to do a little work. Today I received a card from Mama that had been written to me on the 9th of last month. It doesn't contain anything important. After a brief upswing, today I am once again stuck. Worked quite a bit but without hope. We are supposed to head to Russia again in the next few days. I don't much care for our new commander, a first lieutenant, although I have seen him only in passing.

5.10.14.

Today I received a letter from Keynes,* which came to the local regiment headquarters by way of Norway. He writes only to ask

---

* John Maynard Keynes (1883–1946), the famous British economist, who befriended Wittgenstein during his Cambridge years. During the war, Keynes was a little cool toward Wittgenstein, as someone on the enemy side, but it was Keynes who invited Wittgenstein back to Cambridge in 1925 and helped facilitate his return in 1929. The somewhat rocky friendship between the two lasted all of Wittgenstein's life.

wie es mit Johnson's Geld nach dem Kriege werden wird. Der Brief
hat mir einen Stich gegeben denn es schmerzt einen Geschäftsbrief
von einem zu kriegen mit dem man früher gut gestanden ist; und
gar in dieser Zeit.— Soeben erhielt ich eine Karte von Mama vom
ersten des Monats. Alles wohl! Nun also! – Dachte in den letzten
Tagen oft an Russell. Ob er noch an mich denkt? Es war <u>doch</u> merkwürdig, unser Zusammentreffen! In den Zeiten des äußeren Wohlergehens denken wir nicht an die Ohnmacht des Fleisches; denkt
man aber an die Zeit der Not dann kommt sie einem zum Bewußt-
sein. Und man wendet sich zum Geist. —.

6.10.14.

Gestern ziemlich viel gearbeitet. Der Mensch darf nicht vom
Zufall abhängen. Weder von günstigen noch von ungünstigen.
Gestern kam der neue Kommandant auf's Schiff. —Jetzt schicken
sie Leute von der Beleuchtungsabteilung hierher auf's Schiff die
beim Reflektor herumpatzen. Sorge dich nicht!! Soeben kam Befehl
nach Rußland abzufahren. Also wird es wieder ernst! Gott mit mir.

7.10.14.

Die Nacht durch nach Rußland gefahren; fast gar nicht geschlafen,
Dienst beim Scheinwerfer etc. Wir sollen bald in's Feuer kommen.
Der Geist mit mir. Hier in Szczucin hören wir daß die Russen noch
80 Kilometer weit entfernt seien aber wir haben Anzeichen daß hier
in der Nähe schon etwas los ist. Wir stehen in der Mündung der Wisloka (abends). Es ist mir eisig kalt—von innen. Ich habe jenes gewisse

me what should be done with Johnson's* money after the war. The letter stung me, for it hurts to get a business letter from someone to whom one once felt close; and especially at this time.— Just now I received a card from Mama from the first of the month. All's well. Now then! – Thought about Russell[2] often these last days. I wonder if he still thinks of me? It was really <u>odd</u>, how we came to meet! In times of external well-being, we don't think about the weakness of the flesh; but if the time is one of need, we become conscious of it. And one turns to the spirit. —.

6.10.14.

Yesterday worked quite a bit. Man must not depend on chance. Whether it is favorable or unfavorable. Yesterday the new commander arrived aboard. —Now they are sending people from the lighting division to come up and mess around with the searchlight. Do not upset yourself!! Just now the order came to take off for Russia. So it's becoming serious again. God be with me.

7.10.14.

Sailing on toward Russia all night; had almost no sleep. On duty at the searchlight etc. We are soon to come under fire. May the spirit be with me. Here in Szczucin** we are hearing that the Russians are still 80 kilometers away but there are signs that something is going on nearby. We are standing at the mouth of the Wisloka (evening). I am ice cold—inside. I have that certain feeling:

---

* W. E. Johnson (1858–1931), Cambridge logician, for whom L.W. had funded an annual stipendium, so as to reduce his teaching load.
** See map of Vistula River Valley, p. 26. Not all of the villages in question are marked on the map but all are either en route or back to Cracow along the Vistula or its tributaries.

Gefühl: wenn ich mich nur noch einmal ausschlafen könnte ehe die Geschichte anfängt. ——! Besseres Befinden. Wenig gearbeitet. Ich verstehe es noch immer nicht meine Pflicht nur zu tun weil es meine Pflicht ist und meinen ganzen Menschen für das geistige Leben zu reservieren. Ich kann in einer Stunde sterben, ich kann in zwei Stunden sterben, ich kann in einem Monat sterben oder erst in ein paar Jahren; ich kann es nicht wissen & nichts dafür oder dagegen tun: So ist dies Leben. Wie muß ich also leben um in jenem Augenblick zu bestehen. Im Guten & Schönen zu leben bis das Leben von selbst aufhört.

8.10.14.

Fahren weiter gegen Sandomierz zu. Die Nacht war ruhig; ich sehr müde & schlief fest. Stehen jetzt bei Tarnobrzeg & fahren in anderthalb Stunden gegen Sandomierz. Wenn ich müde bin & mir ist kalt dann verliere ich leider bald den Mut das Leben zu ertragen wie es ist. Aber ich bemühe mich ihn nicht zu verlieren. ——. Jede Stunde des leiblichen Wohlergehens ist eine Gnade.

9.10.14.

Ruhige Nacht. In der Ferne fortwährender Kanonendonner. Stehen noch immer bei Tarnobrzeg. Hier in der Nähe findet offenbar eine enorme Schlacht statt, da man schon seit über 12 Stunden ununterbrochenen Geschützdonner hört; unsere neue Besatzung ist viel besser (netter & anständiger) als die alte. Befehl: alles bewaffnet auf dem Deck antreten. Gott mit mir!— Nach Sandomierz gefahren. Hören fortwährenden starken Geschützdonner & sehen die Granaten explodieren. Ich bin sehr guter Stimmung.—! Den ganzen Tag heftigste Kanonade. Viel gearbeitet; es ist mir noch zum mindesten ein grundlegender Gedanke aussständig. ——.

if only I could have one good night's sleep before action begins!
——! Feeling better. I worked a little. I still do not understand
how to do my duty just because it is my duty and to reserve my
entire being for the spiritual life. I may die in an hour, I may die
in two hours, I may die in a month or only in a few years; I can't
know it and can't do anything either for or against it. <u>That's how
life is</u>. How then must I live so as to be prepared for that moment?
One must live for the good and the beautiful until life ends of its
own accord.

8.10.14.

Proceeding further toward Sandomierz [see the map on p. 26]. The
night was quiet; <u>I was very</u> tired & slept soundly. We've now stopped
at Tarnobrzeg & continuing in one-and-a half hours to Sandomierz.
When I am tired & cold, I soon lose the strength to bear life as it
is. But I am trying not to lose my nerve. —. Every hour of physical
well being is a blessing.

9.10.14.

Quiet night. In the distance continuous cannon fire. We are still
in Tarnobrzeg. Here nearby there is evidently a huge battle taking place, since for more than 12 hours, we could hear uninterrupted gunfire; our new crew is <u>much</u> better (nicer & more decent)
than the old one. Command: everyone armed and up on deck!. God
be with me!— Continued to Sandomierz. We constantly hear loud
gunfire & see the grenades exploding. I am in a very good mood.
—! All day the heaviest cannon fire. Worked a great deal; there is
at least <u>one</u> groundbreaking thought pending. —.

10.10.14.

Ruhige Nacht. Früh die Kanonade wieder aufgenommem. Sollen jetzt weiter nach Zawichost fahren. Stehen in Nadbrzezie. Ich schlafe gerade an der Wand der Kajüte unseres Kommandanten und habe ein Gespräch der Zugsführer mit ihm belauscht: Wir sollen den Übergang über die Weichsel für die Deutschen formieren helfen. Er sagte wir hätten kein Artilleriefeuer sondern nur Infanteriefeuer zu erwarten. Viel gearbeitet aber ohne positiven Erfolg. Es ist mir als läge mir ein Gedanke schon fast auf der Zunge. —!

11.10.14.

Ruhige Nacht. — Trage die "Darlegung des Evangeliums" von Tolstoi <u>immer</u> mit mir herum, wie einen Talisman. Ich belausche wieder ein Gespräch unseres Kommandanten mit dem eines anderen Schiffes: heute sollen wir hier in Nadbrzezie bleiben und erst morgen vielleicht hinunter fahren. Soeben erlausche ich die Nachricht daß Antwerpen gefallen ist! Und irgendwo haben unsere Truppen eine große Schlacht gewonnen. Die Gnade die ich genieße indem ich jetzt denken & arbeiten kann ist unbeschreiblich. Ich muß Gleichgültigkeit gegen die Schwierigkeiten des <u>äußeren</u> Lebens erlangen. Heute nacht sollen wir nach Zawichost fahren um Truppen & Material zu landen; wir müssen gerade vor die russischen Stellungen hinfahren. Gott mit mir. —.

12.10.14.

Sind nicht nach Zawichost gefahren. Ruhige Nacht. Horche wieder: Ein Oberleutnant & 2 Leutnants mit unserem Kommandanten: sie wissen noch nicht bestimmt was sie tun werden aber es ist wahrscheinlich daß wir nach Zawichost fahren. Der fremde Oberleutnant ist sehr ehrgeizig und will durchaus daß wir zur Front kommen. — Es wechseln in mir Zeiten der Gleichgültigkeit gegen

10.10.14.

Quiet night. Early in the morning, the cannon fire began again.
Now we're supposed to proceed on to Zawichost. Still in Nadbrzezie.
My bed is right next to the wall of the commander's cabin and I
overheard a conversation between him and the sergeant: We are
supposed to help the Germans make the crossing over the Vistula. He said we had no artillery fire to expect, only infantry fire.
Worked a lot without positive results. It is as though a thought were
lying right on the tip of my tongue. —!

11.10.14.

Quiet night. — I carry *The Gospel in Brief* by Tolstoy around with
me, <u>always</u>, as if it were a talisman. Again I overhear a conversation
between our commander and another one: today we are supposed
to stay here in Nadbrzezie and perhaps not proceed on down until
tomorrow. Just this minute I overheard the news that we've taken
Antwerp! And somewhere or other our troops have won a big battle.
The grace I've been given to think & work now is indescribable.
I must acquire indifference to the hardships of the <u>external</u> life.
Tonight we are supposed to move on to Zawichost to land troops
& matériel; we must get there right before the Russians establish
their positions. God be with me. ——.

12.10.14.

We did not leave for Zawichost. Quiet night. Again I eavesdrop: A
first lieutenant & two lieutenants with our commander; they don't
yet know for sure where they are to go, but it is likely that we
will go to Zawichost. The visiting first lieutenant is very ambi-
tious and wants us to get to the Front at all costs. — Periods of
indifference alternate inside me with others in which I long for

das äußere Schicksal mit solchen in welchen ich mich wieder nach äußerer Freiheit & Ruhe sehne, wo ich es müde bin willenlos jeden beliebigen Befehl ausführen zu müssen. Über die <u>nächste</u> Zukunft <u>völlig</u> im Ungewissen! Kurz es gibt Zeiten wo ich nicht <u>bloß</u> in der Gegenwart und für den Geiste leben kann. Die guten Stunden des Lebens soll man als Gnade dankbar genießen und sonst gegen das Leben gleichgültig sein. Heute habe ich lange mit einer Depression gekämpft dann nach langer Zeit wieder onaniert & endlich den vorigen Satz geschrieben. Höre soeben daß wir heute nacht das für gestern geplante Unternehmen ausführen werden. Davon daß wir nach Krakau kommen ist noch gar keine Rede. Also heute nacht! —! Wir sollen mit Schnellfeuerkanonen & Maschinengewehren schießen wie ich höre, mehr um Lärm zu machen als zu treffen. Auch entnehme ich daß die Sache gefährlich werden wird. Wenn ich mit dem Scheinwerfer leuchten soll so bin ich <u>gewiß</u> verloren. Aber das macht nichts denn nur eines ist nötig! In einer Stunde fahren wir ab. <u>Gott ist mit mir</u>!

13.10.14.
Um 11½ kam der Befehl daß wir nicht oder doch <u>noch</u> nicht nach Zawichost fahren. Also, ruhige Nacht. Höre soeben daß unsere Schiffe Befehl gekriegt haben <u>sofort</u> die Weichsel hinunter zu fahren.—. Wir fahren bereits. Ich bin Geist & darum bin ich frei. Wir stehen bei Lopiza & die Granaten fliegen über uns weg & pfeifen. Zogen uns nach Nadbrzezie zurück & fahren jetzt wieder auf neuen Befehl an dieselbe Stelle. Den ganzen Nachmittag heftigstes Geschützfeuer. Ich war die ganze Zeit bester Stimmung und von dem Donner wie berauscht. Abends fuhren wir nach Sandomierz wo wir die Nacht über stehen bleiben sollen. —. Viel gearbeitet ———.

external freedom and peace, in which I am tired of having to execute each and every command without a will of my own. I am <u>completely</u> in the dark about my <u>immediate</u> future. In brief, there are times when I cannot live <u>just</u> in the present and for the spirit. One should enjoy the good hours of life gratefully, as a blessing, and otherwise feel indifferent toward life. Today I fought for a long time against depression, then for the first time in ages masturbated & finally wrote the preceding sentence. I am just hearing that tonight we will carry out the maneuver planned for yesterday. There is no mention at all yet of our proceeding on to Kraków. So tonight!—! We are to shoot with rapid-fire cannon and machine guns, so I hear, more as a show of strength than to hit our target. I also gather that the affair may become dangerous. If I have to operate the searchlight I am <u>surely</u> undone. But that doesn't matter since only one thing is necessary! In one hour, we depart. <u>God is with me</u>!

13.10.14.

At 11:30 came the order that we are not, or at least not <u>yet</u>, proceeding to Zawichost. So, a quiet night. I heard just now that our ships have received the command to sail down the Vistula right away—. We are now on our way. I am all spirit & therefore I am free. We are moored at Lopiza & the grenades are flying above us and whistling. We retreated to Nadbrzezie and now we are following a new command to proceed to the same place. All afternoon the heaviest gunfire. I was in the best mood the whole time and as if intoxicated by the thunder. In the evening we headed to Sandomierz where we were to spend the night.—Worked hard ——.

14.10.14.

Ruhige Nacht. Bis abends in Sandomierz gestanden & werden wohl auch noch diese Nacht da stehen. Sehr viel gearbeitet aber nicht sehr befriedigt da es wieder schwer ist den Überblick zu gewinnen. —.

15.10.14.

Ruhige Nacht. Onaniere jetzt etwa einmal in 1½ Wochen. Arbeite wenig manuell, aber dafür um so mehr geistig; gehe um 9 Uhr schlafen & um 6 stehe ich auf. Mit dem jetzigen Kommandanten spreche ich so gut wie nie. Er ist aber wohl nicht allzu schlecht. Standen den ganzen Tag in Sandomierz & werden wohl auch nachts hier bleiben. Sehr viel gearbeitet & nicht ohne Zuversicht. Es scheint mir fast als stünde ich knapp vor einer Lösung. —.

16.10.14.

Früh um 8 nach Szczucin gefahren um Geschütze zu holen.

17.10.14.

Gestern <u>sehr</u> viel gearbeitet; der Knoten zog sich immer mehr zusammen aber ich fand keine Lösung. Abends blieben wir bei Baranow stehen & fahren jetzt um 6 p.m. weiter nach Szczucin. — Ob mir der erlösende Gedanke kommen wird? ob er kommen wird??!! — Gestern & heute onaniert. — Abends in Szczucin angekommen wo wir die Nacht über stehen bleiben werden. <u>Sehr</u> viel gearbeitet. Bin davon etwas angegriffen. <u>Sehr</u> viel Material angehäuft ohne es ordnen zu können. Aber diesen Andrang von Material halte ich für ein gutes Zeichen. Erinnere dich <u>wie</u> groß die Gnade der Arbeit ist! —.

14.10.14.

Quiet night. We stayed at Sandomierz till evening & will probably stay there tonight too. Worked a great deal but not very satisfied because it is once again hard to attain an overview. —.

15.10.14.

Quiet night. I masturbate about once in 1½ weeks now. Do little manual work, but hence all the more mentally active, go to sleep at 9 o'clock & get up at 6. I communicate as little as possible with the current commander. But he is not that bad. Spent the whole day in Sandomierz & will probably stay here tonight too. Worked a great deal & not without confidence. It seems to me almost as if I were approaching a solution. —.

16.10.14.

Went to Szczucin to get artillery supplies at 8 in the morning.

17.10.14.

Yesterday worked <u>very</u> hard; the knot has become steadily less tight but I have found no solution. In the evening we stayed at Baranow and now at 6 p.m. we are continuing on to Szczucin.—Will I find the redemptive thought? Will it come to me??!!—Yesterday & today I masturbated.— We arrived in Szczucin where we will spend the night, in the evening. Worked <u>very</u> hard. I'm a little exhausted by it. Accumulated a <u>huge</u> mass of material without being able to organize it. Yet I take this overload of material to be a good sign. Remember <u>how</u> great the blessing of work is!—

18.10.14.

Vormittag einkaufen. Um Mittag fuhren wir nach Tarnobrzeg ab. 5 p.m. in Tarnobrzeg. Wenig gearbeitet. Gegen abend kamen Offiziere aufs Schiff um es anzuschauen. Ich kam mit einem in's Gespräch dem mein Freiwilligenabzeichen auffiel. Wir sprachen über eine Stunde mit einander sehr gemütlich. Er war sehr freundlich & nicht dumm. Er trug mir das "Du" an, was mich freute. Wenig gearbeitet aber das macht nichts! – Bleiben über Nacht in Tarnobrzeg.——.

19.10.14.

Früh nach Sandomierz gefahren wo wir jetzt stehen. Nachts wieder onaniert (halb im Traum). Das kommt daher daß ich wenig, fast gar keine Bewegung mache. Nachmittag wieder nach Tarnobrzeg gefahren. Bin seit gestern mit meiner Verdauung nicht ganz in der Ordnung. — Die Lösung des Problems liegt mir auf der Zunge! — Gegen abend wieder nach Sandomierz. Fühle mich nicht recht wohl, keine echte Lebenslust. —! Sehr viel gearbeitet.—.

20.10.14.

Unwohl. Sehr viel gearbeitet. Nachmittag besseres Befinden. Bin aber nicht recht glücklich; habe Sehnsucht nach David: Wenn ich ihm wenigstens schreiben könnte. Aber mein Geist spricht in mir gegen meine Depression. Gott mit mir. —.

21.10.14.

Es heißt wir sollen wieder nach Krakau fahren; das wäre mir nicht unangenehm. —. Stehen den ganzen Tag hier in Sandomierz. Sehr viel & mit Zuversicht gearbeitet. Abends etwas müde & in diesem Zustand bin ich Depressionen recht zugänglich; aber, nur Mut! —

18.10.14.

In the morning, shopping. At noon we sailed to Tarnobrzeg, in Tarnobrzeg by 5 p.m. I worked very little. Toward evening officers
came aboard for an inspection. I got into a conversation with one
of them who noticed my volunteer stripes. We chatted, very pleas-
antly, for over an hour. He was very friendly and not stupid. He
addressed me as "Du," which pleased me. Worked little but that
doesn't matter! – Staying overnight in Tarnobrzeg.———.

19.10.14.

In the morning sailed for Sandomierz where we are now. At night
masturbated again (while half asleep). This is happening because I
am getting so little, almost no exercise. In the afternoon we again
moved on to Tarnobrzeg. My digestion has not quite been in order
since yesterday. — The solution to the problem is on the tip of my
tongue! — Toward evening, back to Sandomierz. Don't feel quite
right, no real zest for life. —! Worked very hard.—

20.10.14.

Unwell. Worked <u>very</u> hard. In the afternoon I felt better. But I am
not really happy; I am longing for David: if only I could at least
write him. But my spirit speaks within me countering my depression. May God be with me. —.

21.10.14.

The word is that we are supposed to go to Kraków again; that would
not displease me. —. We are staying all day here in Sandomierz. I
worked very hard & with confidence. A little tired in the evening &
in that condition where I am quite prone to depression; but I must
have courage! —.

22.10.14.

Die Gefechte hier in der Nähe dauern fort. Gestern starke Kanonade. Viel gearbeitet. Den ganzen Tag gestanden. —.

23.10.14.

Fahren jetzt, vormittags, nach Tarnobrzeg. Arbeite <u>sehr</u> fleißig
aber noch ohne Erfolg. Abends wieder in Sandomierz. <u>Sehr</u> viel
gearbeitet. Denke viel an David. Ob ich ihn noch einmal sehen
werde? —! —.

24.10.14.

Schlecht geschlafen. (Zu wenig Bewegung!). Unser Kommandant
ist sehr mäßig; hochmütig unfreundlich & behandelt jeden als
seinen Diener. Nachmittag nach Tarnobrzeg wo wir diese Nacht
bleiben. Sehr viel gearbeitet zwar noch ohne Erfolg aber mit viel
Zuversicht. Ich <u>belagere</u> jetzt mein Problem. —.

25.10.14.

Früh nach Sandomierz. Gestern abends kam uns die unsinnige
Nachricht zu Paris sei gefallen. Auch ich war übrigens zuerst erfreut
bis ich die Unmöglichkeit der Nachricht einsah. Solche unmögli-
chen Nachrichten sind immer ein sehr schlechtes Zeichen. Wenn
wirklich etwas für uns Günstiges vorfällt dann wird <u>das</u> berichtet
& niemand verfällt auf solche Absurditäten. Fühle darum heute
mehr als je die furchtbare Traurigkeit unserer—der deutschen

22.10.14.

Fighting close by here is constantly going on. There was strong cannon fire yesterday. I worked a great deal. Was able to stand it all day. —.

23.10.14.

Now sailing this morning for Tarnobrzeg. I am working very diligently but still without success. Again in Sandomierz in the evening. I worked a great deal. Thinking a lot about David. Will I ever see him again? —! —.

24.10.14.

I slept badly. (Too little activity!). Our commander is very mediocre; arrogant, unfriendly & treats everyone as his servant. We are staying tonight in Tarnobrzeg, where we went in the afternoon. Worked a great deal, still with no success but with confidence. I am laying siege to my problem. —.

25.10.14.

In the morning to Sandomierz. Last night we received the suspicious news that Paris had fallen. Even I was pleased at first, until I understood the absurdity of the dispatch. Such incredible news is always a bad sign. When anything positive really happens to us, it is announced & no one falls for such absurd stories. So I feel today, more than ever, the terrible sadness of our—the

Rasse—Lage!! Denn daß wir gegen England nicht aufkommen können scheint mir so gut wie gewiß: Die Engländer—die beste Rasse der Welt—<u>können</u> nicht verlieren! Wir aber können verlieren & werden verlieren, wenn nicht in diesem Jahr so im nächsten! Der Gedanke daß unsere Rasse geschlagen werden soll deprimiert mich furchtbar denn ich bin ganz & gar deutsch!

Werden plötzlich durch Gewehrfeuer von den Russen

Gott mit mir!— Es war nichts als ein russischer Aeroplan.

—,— Sehr viel gearbeitet. Stehen die Nacht über in Tarnobrzeg & fahren morgen früh gegen Szczucin. Gegen Mittag wich meine Depression —.

26.10.14.

Früh gegen Szczucin. Fahren den ganzen Tag über. Habe Kopfschmerzen & bin müde. Trotzdem viel gearbeitet.—.

27.10.14.

Früh gegen Szczucin weiter gefahren. Sehr viel gearbeitet. Heute nacht habe ich Wachdienst. —.

28.10.14.

Vor-& nachmittag wegen sehr großer Müdigkeit fast unfähig zu arbeiten. Schlief in der Nacht so gut wie nichts. Der größte Teil der

German race's*—position!! That we cannot prevail over England strikes me as good as certain: the English—the best race in the world—<u>cannot</u> lose! We, however, can lose & will lose, if not this year, then the next! The thought that our race will be defeated depresses me terribly because I am German through & through!

Suddenly, we are being subjected to gunfire by the Russians

God be with me!— It was nothing but a Russian airplane. — , —. I worked very hard. We are spending the night in Tarnobrzeg & will go on tomorrow morning to Szczucin. Toward noon my depression lifted —.

26.10.14.

Early morning on toward Szczucin. Sailing all day. Have a headache & am tired. Just the same I worked a lot.—.

27.10.14.

Early morning further toward Szczucin. Worked a great deal. But tonight I am on duty. —.

28.10.14.

Morning & afternoon almost unable to work because of great fatigue. Sleep at night hopeless. The majority of the crew was drunk

---

* The reference, in this often-cited passage, to nationhood as *race*, which is bound to strike contemporary readers as offensive, was, as other writings of the period testify, not at all uncommon. "Race" was often used interchangeably with nation, as in "the French race." Such phrases remained in the vocabulary until the Nazis began to refer to the Germans as "the Master Race." After World War II, the usage wholly disappeared.

Wittgenstein's insistence here that he is "German through and through" is more of a momentary exclamation than a real conviction: Wittgenstein did not mourn for a lost Austria (and certainly not Germany!) at war's end and looked to England for much of his intellectual support.

Mannschaft war besoffen so daß meine Wache recht unangenehm war. Fuhren früh gegen Sandomierz. Auf dem Wege brach ein Schaufelrad. Wir müssen nach Krakau von einem anderen Schiff geschleppt werden. Auf der Fahrt nach Krakau. Erhielt heute viel Post u.a. die traurige Nachricht daß Paul schwer verwundet & in russischer Gefangenschaft ist — Gott sei Dank in guter Pflege. Die arme, arme, Mama!!!— —. — Auch von Ficker & der Jolles liebe Nachtricht. Endlich einen Brief aus Norwegen worin Draegni much um 1000 Kronen bittet. Aber ob ich sie ihm senden kann? Jetzt wo Norwegen sich unseren Feinden angeschlossen hat!!! Dies ist übrigens auch eine furchtbar traurige Tatsache. Immer wieder muß ich an den armen Paul denken der so plötzlich um seinen Beruf gekommen ist! Wie furchtbar. Welche Philosophie würde es bedürfen darüber hinweg zu kommen! Wenn dies überhaupt anders als durch Selbstmord geschehen kann!! — Konnte nicht viel arbeiten, arbeite aber mit Zuversicht. ——. Dein Wille geschehe. — —.

29.10.14.

Auf dem Weg nach Krakau. Blieben stehen weil unser Schlepper nach Sandomierz zurück mußte. Warten bis er zurückkommt. Vormitags Kopfschmerzen und Müdigkeit. Dachte viel an Paul. Sehr viel gearbeitet. Belagere noch immer mein Problem, habe schon viele Forts genommen. Sehe jetzt so klar und ruhig wie nur in den besten Zeiten. Wenn ich nur diesmal alles Wesentliche lösen könnte, ehe die Gute Zeit um ist!!! ——.

so that my watch was quite unpleasant. Sailed early to Sandomierz. On the way a paddle wheel broke. To get to Kraków we have to be towed by another ship. On the way now to Kraków. Received a lot of mail today, among other things the sad news that Paul* was seriously wounded & in Russian captivity — thank God in good care. Poor, poor Mama!!!— —. — I also received warm messages from von Ficker & Frau Jolles. Finally a letter from Norway in which Draegni** begs me for 1000 Kronen. But will I be able to send them to him? Now that Norway has allied itself with our enemy!!!*** This is by the way a terribly sad state of affairs as well. Again and again, I have to think of poor Paul, who has so suddenly been <u>deprived of his vocation</u>! How terrible! What philosophical outlook would it take to overcome such a thing? Can it even happen except through suicide!! — I couldn't work much, but work with assurance. ——. Thy will be done. — —.

29.10.14.

On the way to Kraków. We remained moored because our tow had to return to Sandomierz. We are waiting till it returns. In the morning, headache & fatigue. I thought a lot of Paul. Worked a great deal. I still attack my problem, have already taken many forts. I now see so clearly & calmly as one does only in the best of times. If I could only solve all the essentials before the good time is over!!! ——.

---

* Paul Wittgenstein (1887–1961), Wittgenstein's older brother, who had just lost his right arm in battle. After the war, he resumed his career as concert pianist, commissioning pieces that could be played with one hand.

** Halvard Draegni, factory owner in the village of Skjolden, Norway, with whose family Wittgenstein stayed in 1913.

*** Here Wittgenstein got his facts wrong: Norway remained neutral in World War I.

30.10.14.

Erhielten heute eine deutsche Zeitung. Keine guten Nachrichten, was so viel heißt als schlechte Nachrichten! Es ist <u>schwer</u> zu arbeiten, wenn solche Gedanken einen stören!! Habe trotzdem auch am Nachmittag gearbeitet. Ich empfinde oft schwer, daß ich hier niemand habe, mit dem ich mich etwas aussprechen kann. Aber ich will mich <u>allen</u> Gewalten zum Trotze erhalten.

30.10.14.

We received a German newspaper today. No good news which is to say bad news! It is <u>hard</u> to work when such thoughts distract you!! Nevertheless I worked in the afternoon. I often find it difficult that I don't have anyone here with whom I can discuss things. But "in defiance of all threats, I will remain firm."*

---

* The last sentence alludes to J. W. von Goethe's poem "Lila" (1777), which contains the rhyming lines "Allen Gewalten / Zum Trutz sich erhalten / Nimmer sich beugen, / Kräftig sich zeigen . . ." "In defiance of all threats / To remain firm. / Never to bend. / To show one's strength."

NOTEBOOK 2

October 30, 1914–June 22, 1915

EDITOR'S NOTE

A S THE WINTER of 1915 set in, Wittgenstein experienced what can only be called his Dark Night of the Soul. In the opening pages of Notebook 2, he is still "working hard," using the language of war metaphorically to describe his work: "Lay siege to the problem with <u>desperate</u> urgency. But I would rather spill my blood before this fortress than withdraw empty-handed." And again, "until the city has fallen, one cannot forever rest in one of its forts." Tackling the riddles of logic was like the siege of a walled city.

The *Goplana* was scheduled to arrive in Kraków by early November, and Wittgenstein was looking forward eagerly to visiting the poet Georg Trakl, who was a patient in the garrison hospital there. Before the war, Wittgenstein had made a very generous financial bequest to a group of poets and artists chosen by Ludwig von Ficker, the editor of *Der Brenner*, from artists in need. These included Trakl as well as Rainer Marie Rilke and the architect Adolf Loos. Wittgenstein had never met Trakl and knew little about contemporary poetry, yet somehow he considered Trakl a kind of soulmate. But when he arrived in Kraków and went to the hospital, he was informed that the poet had died a few days earlier. "This hit me very hard," Wittgenstein wrote in his notebook, "How sad, how sad!!!"

In the weeks that followed, depression set in, prompted by the fear that, in the meaningless daily round, he was losing his very identity, his soul. "Only not to lose oneself!!!" he prays. And again, "I see myself, the 'I' which I used to be able to inhabit securely, as a desirable distant island that has deserted me." Wittgenstein was reading Nietzsche's *The Antichrist* and remarks, "I am deeply moved by his hostility to Christianity. For there is always some truth in his writings." "Such a life [that of the atheist]," Wittgenstein tells himself, "makes no sense." Yet there is the nagging question, "But why not live a life that makes no sense? Is it unworthy?" And although he reluctantly reminds himself that, unlike Nietzsche, he "must always—be conscious always—of the spirit," one can see that doubt remains.

On December 4, Wittgenstein finally got the transfer he had been waiting for. He was discharged from the *Goplana* and assigned to the artillery workshop in Kraków, where his desk job consisted largely of making inventories of vehicles in use. He was now given a room of his own and was sometimes invited to the officers' dining room. These privileges should have improved Wittgenstein's mood, but the fact is that when things went smoothly, he turned inward and became depressed, whereas when he had to endure cannon fire and possible death, he rallied.

At New Year's, he was informed that his commander, Lieutenant Gürth, wanted to take him along on a quick business trip to Vienna. One would think that Wittgenstein would have welcomed such an invitation, but somehow he did not. Once in Vienna, he spent only a single day with his family and two afternoons with

Warsaw: Artillery workshop, metal workshop, 1916
(Kriegssammlung-Fotos 1914–1918 © Austrian National Library,
Vienna)

their family friend, the pianist Josef Labor. Otherwise, he was presumably with Gürth, but, except for a dinner in Mödling "with a Captain Roth whom I found terribly unappealing," we don't know how the two spent their time. On January 2, Wittgenstein writes cryptically, "I want to remind myself here that my moral standing is now much lower than it was at Easter."

The allusion is probably to some sexual affair, but Wittgenstein never specifies. Once back in Kraków, he is unable to do any serious work and refers frequently to his "unsatisfactory" position at the workshop: "Something will have to happen.—. I have to endure much irritation & insult and am squandering my inner strength. I have strong sexual feelings again and masturbate almost every day: it cannot continue this way—."

Which way? Wittgenstein records frequent trips to the baths and to a café in town but never confides more than these facts even to his private diary. On February 11, he writes, "My relationship with one of the officers—Cadet Adam—is now very tense. It is possible that it may come to a duel between us." We never hear of this duel again; subsequent entries merely allude to depression: "Did no work. Dark mood. Strong sexual desire. Feeling lonely. . . . I have lost all hope and confidence in my power to succeed" (27.2.15). And then again comes the admonition, "Only do not lose yourself!!—.—." A "lovely letter" from David provides some respite but not for long. On April 22, Wittgenstein is made supervisor of the whole artillery workshop, but the promotion doesn't cheer him up. "Did no work" has become a monotonous refrain. For four long months, the philosophy manuscript languishes.

Then suddenly something changes: On April 24, the entries begin to open with the exclamation "Working!" and, before long, we find on the recto page of May 23 the axiom that was to be central to Wittgenstein's later thinking: "*The limits of my language* mean the limits of my world." Now, when he finds his mind opening up, the focus is no longer on the refinement of logic as such, but on the larger questions of life. On June 1, the recto reads:

> The great problem around which everything I write revolves is: Is there a priori an order in the world, and if so, of what does it consist?
>
> You are looking into a fog bank and hence persuade yourself that the goal is near. But the fog lifts, and the goal is not yet in sight.

Not yet in sight, but near. It is a turning point.

17.12.

...unkt auszusprechen sind nicht mehr

...l sonst könnte sie nicht

...erden

18.12.14

...zu unterscheiden und

...soviel zu unterscheiden

...ls am Sachverhalt zu ...

...den ist. Darin besteht die

...tat.

20.12.14

...ist nicht mehr u nicht

...zu erkennen als "..."

...en der Sachverhalt nicht

...eobachtbare und nicht

...cht überschaubaren.

...könnte auch so fragen

...ich zum Zweck der ...

...mit einem Anderen

GERMAN TEXT *of* NOTEBOOK 2

ZWEITES HEFT, MS. 102

30.10.1914–22.6.1915

30.10.14.

(Abends) Erhielt soeben liebe Post. Eine sehr liebe Karte von Frege! Eine von Trakl & Ficker! Mama, Klara, Frau Klingenberg. Dies hat mich sehr gefreut.

Sehr viel gearbeitet. —.

31.10.14.

Heute früh weiter gegen Krakau. Den ganzen Tag gearbeitet. Habe das Problem <u>verzweifelt</u> gestürmt! Aber ich will eher mein Blut vor dieser Festung lassen ehe ich unverrichteter Dinge abziehe. Die größte Schwierigkeit ist die einmal eroberten Forts zu halten bis man ruhig in ihnen sitzen kann. Und bis nicht die <u>Stadt</u> gefallen ist kann man <u>nicht</u> für immer ruhig in einem der Forts sitzen. —.

Heute nacht habe ich Wache und bin leider schon durch das intensive Arbeiten <u>sehr</u> müde. Meine Arbeit noch immer ohne Erfolg! Nur zu! —. Stehen heute nacht in Szczucin. —.

ENGLISH TEXT *of* NOTEBOOK 2

SECOND NOTEBOOK, MS. 102

30.10.1914–22.6.1915

30.10.14.

(Evening) Just received nice mail. A very kind card from Frege! One from Trakl & Ficker! Mama, Klara, Frau Klingenberg. This pleased me very much.

Worked very hard.——.

31.10.14.

Sailed further toward Kraków this morning. Worked all day. Lay siege to the problem with <u>desperate</u> urgency. But I would rather spill my blood before this fortress than withdraw empty-handed. The greatest difficulty is to hold on to those fortresses you have already captured until you can sit quietly inside one of them. And until the town has fallen, you cannot forever rest in one of its forts.——.

I have watch duty tonight and am already <u>very</u> tired from the intensive work. My work is still unsuccessful! Keep on!——. Tonight we are staying in Szczucin.——.

1.11.14.

Vormittag weiter gegen Krakau. Während des Wachdienstes heute nacht gearbeitet, auch heute sehr viel und noch immer erfolglos. Bin aber nicht mutlos weil ich das <u>Hauptproblem</u> immer im Auge habe. —. Trakl liegt im Garnisonsspital in Krakau und bittet mich ihn zu besuchen. Wie gerne möchte ich ihn kennen lernen! Hoffentlich treffe ich ihn wenn ich nach Krakau komme! Vielleicht wäre es mir eine große Stärkung. —.

2.11.14.

Früh weiter gegen Krakau. Bin wieder sinnlicher. Gegen abend wieder am Sand stecken geblieben. Es ist bitter kalt. Es ist wirklich ein Glück daß man sich selbst hat & immer zu sich flüchten kann. Viel gearbeitet. Die Gnade der Arbeit!! —.

3.11.14.

Früh weiter gegen Krakau. Höre daß die Russen wieder vorgerückt sind und 20 km von Opatowiec stehen; wir stehen 10 km von dort. —. Was wird jetzt mit mir geschehen wenn ich nahe Krakau komme?!? Fast den ganzen Tag gearbeitet. —. Werden wahrscheinlich heute nacht fahren. Hören Kanonendonner & sehen den Blitz. — ! —.

4.11.14.

Ruhige Nacht. Früh weiter. Sehr viel gearbeitet. Morgen sollen wir in Krakau sein. Höre daß wir wahrscheinlich eine Belagerung von Krakau zu erwarten haben. Da werde ich viel Kraft brauchen um den Geist zu bewahren. —. Häng nur nicht von der äußeren Welt ab dann brauchst du dich vor dem was in ihr geschieht nicht zu fürchten. Heute nacht Wachdienst. Es ist leichter von Dingen als von Menschen unabhängig zu sein. Aber auch das muß man können! —.

1.11.14.

Further toward Kraków this morning. Worked during watch duty last night and again today a great deal and still without success. But I am not discouraged because I always have my eye on the <u>central problem</u>. —. Trakl is lying in the garrison hospital in Kraków and begs me to come visit him. How anxious I am to get to know him! Hopefully I will meet him when I get to Kraków! Perhaps it would give me a big lift. —.

2.11.14.

On to Kraków this morning. Once again feeling more sexually aroused. In the evening, the ship got stuck in the sand again. It is bitterly cold. It is really fortunate to have one's self & that one can always withdraw into the self. Worked a great deal. The blessing of work!!!—.

3.11.14.

On to Kraków this morning. I hear that the Russians have again made advances and are now 20 km from Opatowiec; we are 10 km from there.—. What will happen to me now when I get closer to Kraków?!? Worked almost all day.—. We will probably proceed tonight. I hear cannon thunder and see the lightning flash. —!—.

4.11.14.

Quiet night. We sailed further this morning. Worked a great deal. Tomorrow we're supposed to be in Kraków. I hear that we can probably expect an attack in Kraków. So I will need much strength to preserve the spirit.—. Be sure not to be dependent on the external world, then you don't need to be afraid of what takes place in it. Watch duty tonight. It is easier to detach oneself from things than from people. But even that is something one must master!—.

5.11.14.

Früh weiter nach Krakau wo wir spät abends ankommen sollen. Bin sehr gespannt ob ich Trakl treffen werde. Ich hoffe es sehr. Ich vermisse sehr einen Menschen mit dem ich mich ein wenig ausreden kann. Es wird auch ohne einen solchen gehen müssen. Aber es würde mich sehr stärken. Den ganzen Tag etwas müde & zur Depression geneigt. Nicht sehr viel gearbeitet.

    In Krakau. Es ist schon zu spät Trakl heute noch zu besuchen. —— Möge der Geist mir Kraft geben. ——

6.11.14.

Früh in die Stadt zum Garnisonsspital. Erfuhr dort daß Trakl vor wenigen Tagen gestorben ist! Dies traf mich <u>sehr</u> stark. Wie traurig, wie traurig!!! Ich schrieb darüber sofort an Ficker. Besorgungen gemacht & dann gegen 6′ Uhr aufs Schiff gekommen. Nicht gearbeitet. Der arme Trakl! —! Dein Wille geschehe. ——

7.11.14.

Gestern um neun Uhr abends kam plötzlich der Befehl für eine Arbeit an einem anderen Schiff mit dem Scheinwerfer zu leuchten. Also aus dem Bett heraus und bis 3½ früh geleuchtet. Bin in Folge dessen sehr müde. Nachmittag in der Stadt auf Besorgungen. Die Belagerung von Krakau wird jetzt mit aller Bestimmtheit erwartet. Ich will trachten von diesem Schiff wegzukommen. Nicht gearbeitet. Ich sehne mich nach einem anständigen Menschen denn

5.11.14.

Morning, closer to Kraków where we should arrive late this evening. I am very anxious to know if I shall meet Trakl. I very much hope so. I really miss having someone with whom I can have a real conversation. Even without one, it will be alright. But it would greatly fortify me. All day a little tired & prone to depression. Didn't do much work.

Now in Kraków. It is too late tonight to visit Trakl.——. May the spirit give me strength.——

6.11.14.

Into the city to the garrison hospital early this morning. Found out that Trakl had died there a few days ago!!* This hit me <u>very</u> hard. How sad, how sad!!! I wrote to Ficker about it right away. Ran a few errands & then at about 6 o'clock came back aboard. Did no work. Poor poor Trakl!——.! Thy will be done.——

7.11.14.

There suddenly came a request yesterday at nine o'clock in the evening to take the searchlight to another ship that needed lighting. So I got out of bed and provided illumination until 3:30 this morning. As a result, I am very tired. This afternoon I went into the city to make some purchases. The siege of Kraków** is now expected with all certainty. I must try to get away from this ship. I have done no work. I am longing for the company of a decent person because

---

* Trakl had been working as an orderly in the military hospital at Kraków; Ficker had arranged for him to meet Wittgenstein. Trakl, who was only twenty-seven, had died a few days earlier, supposedly of a heart attack but more likely of a drug overdose.
** In 1914 Kraków (now belonging to Poland) was a bustling city of 150,000, with beautiful buildings designed by Viennese architects, a modern system of trams, and good theaters and concert halls.

hier bich ich von <u>Unanständikeit</u> <u>umringt</u>. Möge der Geist mich nicht verlassen und in mir beständiger werden.————.

8.11.14.

Bin nicht recht zum Arbeiten gestimmt. Lese viel. Heute nacht Wachdienst. Fast nichts gearbeitet. Bin etwas über meine Zukunft besorgt. —.

9.11.14.

Belauschte eben ein Gespräch unseres Kommandanten mit einem anderen Offizier: Was für gemeine Stimmen. Die ganze Schlechtigkeit der Welt kreischt & krächzt aus ihnen heraus. Gemeinheit wo ich hinsehe. <u>Kein</u> fühlendes Herz soweit mein Auge reicht!!! ——

Erhalte eine <u>sehr</u> liebe Karte von Onkel Paul. So eine Karte sollte mich erfrischen & stärken aber ich bin in den letzten Tagen <u>deprimierbar</u>!! Ich habe an nichts eine rechte Freude. Und ich lebe in Angst vor der Zukunft! Weil ich nicht mehr in mir ruhe. Jede Unanständigkeit meiner Umgebung—und solche gibt es immer— verwundet mich im Innersten und ehe eine Wunde verheilt kommt eine frische! Selbst dann wenn—wie jetzt, abends—ich nicht deprimiert bin, fühle ich mich doch nicht so recht frei. Ich habe nur selten & dann ganz vorübergehende Lust zum Arbeiten. Da ich nicht zu einem behaglichen Gefühle kommen kann. Ich fühle mich abhängig von der Welt & muß sie daher auch dann fürchten wenn augenblicklich mir nichts Schlechtes widerfährt. Ich sehe mich selbst, das Ich worin ich sicher ruhen konnte wie ein ersehntes fernes Eiland das von mir gewichen ist.—Die Russen rücken schnell gegen Krakau vor. Die ganze Zivilbevölkerung muß die

here I am <u>surrounded by indecency</u>. May the spirit not leave me and may it become more constant in me.————.

8.11.14.

Am not quite in the mood for work. Reading a great deal. Watch duty tonight. Have done almost no work. A little worried about my future.—.

9.11.14.

Just overheard a conversation between our commander and another officer. What vulgar voices! All the nastiness of the world screeches and croaks out of their mouths. Insolence wherever I look. <u>Not</u> a feeling heart as far as my eye can reach!!!———

Received a very kind card from Uncle Paul.* Such a card should refresh & strengthen me but in the last few days I have been <u>prone to depression</u>!! I take no real pleasure in anything. And I live in fear of the future! Because I am no longer at peace with myself. Every indecency around me—and there are always such—wounds me to the quick and before the wound can heal, there is a new one! Even when—like now, in the evening—I am not depressed, I still don't feel quite right. Only occasionally, and even then quite in passing, do I have a desire to work. Because I cannot find a way to feel comfortable. I feel dependent on the external world & must therefore be afraid of it even when there is no immediate threat to me. I see myself, the I which I used to be able to inhabit securely, as a longed for but distant island that has deserted me.—The Russians are advancing quickly on Kraków. The entire civilian population

---

* Paul Wittgenstein (1842–1928), Wittgenstein's paternal uncle, to whom, along with the late David Pinsent, Wittgenstein dedicated an early version of the *Tractatus* in 1918. In the 1922 version, the name is replaced by those of David Pinsent and Bertrand Russell.

Stadt verlassen. Es sieht mit unserer Sache sehr schlecht aus! <u>Gott steh mir bei</u>!!! Ein wenig gearbeitet.

10.11.14.

Wieder mehr gearbeitet. Und besserer Stimmung. Erfuhr heute daß ich über die Schweiz nach England schreiben könne; gleich morgen werde ich an David & vielleicht an Russell schreiben. Oder vielleicht schon heute. — Ich hoffe jetzt wieder besser arbeiten zu können! —!!

11.11.14.

Netten Brief von Ficker. Ziemlich viel gearbeitet. Wir hörten schon Kanonendonner von den Werken! Habe einen Brief an David abgeschickt. Wie oft ich an ihn denke! Ob er halb so viel an mich denkt? (?)

Heute besserer Stimmung.—!

12.11.14.

Nur sich selbst nicht verlieren!!! Sammle dich! Und arbeite nicht zum Zeitvertreib sondern fromm um zu leben! Tue keinem ein Unrecht! — Es wird von einer 6–7 monatlichen Belagerung gesprochen! Alle Geschäfte sind geschlossen & öffnen nur auf ganz kurze Zeit. Je ernster die Lage wird desto roher werden die Unteroffiziere. Denn sie fühlen daß sie jetzt ungestraft ihre ganze Gemeinheit entladen können da jetzt die Offiziere den Kopf verlieren & im guten Sinn keine Kontrolle mehr ausüben. Jedes Wort was man jetzt hört ist eine Grobheit. Denn die Anständigkeit lohnt sich auf keine Weise mehr und die Leute geben daher auch das bißchen preis was sie etwa noch besitzen. Es ist alles tief traurig.

Nachmittag in der Stadt. Ziemlich viel gearbeitet <u>aber ohne</u>

must leave the city. Our affairs seem to me to be going very badly. God protect me!!! I worked a little.

10.11.14.

Worked some more again. And in a better mood. I found out today that I could write to England via Switzerland; immediately tomorrow I will write to David & perhaps to Russell. Or perhaps already today.—I hope now to work better again! —!!

11.11.14.

Nice letter from Ficker. Worked quite a bit. We heard cannon fire from the workshop. Sent off a letter to David. How often I think of him! I wonder if he thinks of me half as much? (?)

Today in better spirits.—!

12.11.14.

Only not to lose oneself!!! Pull yourself together! And don't work just to pass the time but devoutly so as to live! Do no one an injustice!—. There is talk of a 6–7 month siege! All the shops are closed & they open only for short periods of time. The more serious the situation, the ruder the non-commissioned officers. For they feel that now they can discharge all their villainy without going punished, since the officers are losing their heads & no longer, in a positive sense, exercising any control. Every word you hear now is some insult. For decency no longer gets you anywhere, and people attach no value to whatever remnant of it they might still have. It is all very sad.

Afternoon in town. Worked quite hard but without any real

rechte Klarheit des Sehens! Ob ich noch weiter werde arbeiten können?(!) Ob der Vorhang schon fällt?? Es wäre merkwürdig da ich
inmitten eines Problems stecke, inmitten einer Belagerung. —. —!

13.11.14.
Den ganzen Vormittag habe ich mich vergebens bemüht zu arbeiten. Das klare Sehen will sich nicht einstellen. Denke viel über
mein Leben nach und dies ist auch ein Grund weshalb ich nicht
arbeiten kann. Oder ist es umgekehrt? Ich glaube jetzt daß ich mich
noch immer nicht genug von den anderen am Schiff abschließe.
Ich kann mit ihnen nicht verkehren da mir die gewisse Gemeinheit fehlt die dazu nötig ist. Aber auf ganz unbegreiflicher Weise
fällt mir dies Abschließen nicht leicht. Nicht daß ich mich zu
irgend einem Menschen im geringsten hingezogen fühlte. Aber die
Gewohnheit mit Menschen freundlich zu reden ist so stark!
    Heute nacht Dienst. Gehe jetzt jeden Abend in ein Kaffeehaus
& trinke 2 Gläser Kaffee; & die wohlanständige Atmosphär tut mir
gut. Wenig gearbeitet! —! Gott gebe mir Vernunft & Kraft!!! —.

14.11.14.
Nachts auf der Wache fast die ganze Zeit Vorschriften für mein
Leben mir ausgedacht daß es halbwegs erträglich werde. Bin
grundlos deprimiert, d.h. es fehlt mir zum mindesten jede Lebens-
freude. Und jedes laute Wort das ich höre tut mir weh. Ganz ohne
Grund!! — Auch gearbeitet habe ich heute nacht am Posten. —
    Als eine Gnade muß ich es noch betrachten daß ich in mei-
ner Kammer ruhig sitzen kann & so doch Gelegenheit habe mich
etwas zu sammeln. —Sehr wenig gearbeitet. Tagsüber sehr müde,
wie jetzt leider oft! Nachmittag verging die starke Depression aber
ich war zu müde zum Arbeiten. Abends wie gewöhnlich aus. —!

<u>clarity of vision</u>! Will I be able to do any further work?(!). Is the curtain already coming down?? It would be strange if I were to be stuck inside a problem, in the middle of an attack.—.—!

13.11.14.

I've been trying in vain to work all morning. I can't arrive at a clear picture. I am thinking a great deal about my life and that is also a reason why I cannot work. Or is it the other way around? I now think that I am still not distancing myself enough from the others on the ship. I cannot get along with them because I lack the particular insensitivity that is necessary. But for reasons I find totally incomprehensible, putting an end to the situation is also not easy for me. Not that I feel even remotely drawn to a single person here. But the habit of polite conversation is so engrained in me!

Watch duty tonight. I now go every evening to a café and drink two cups of coffee; & the respectable atmosphere does me good. Have worked very <u>little</u> !—! God give me sanity and strength!!!—

14.11.14.

Spent practically the entire time on duty at night thinking up precepts that would make my life halfway tolerable. I'm depressed for no reason, that is, at the very least I am devoid of all joie de vivre. And every loud word I hear hurts me. Quite without cause!!— I even worked today after my night on duty—

One <u>blessing</u> I should note is that I can sit quietly in my room & so I do have occasion to pull myself together a little.—Did very little work. During the day I was very tired, as is often the case now. In the afternoon the severe depression passed but I was too tired to work. As usual I go out in the evening.—!

15.11.14.

Lese jetzt in Emersons Essays. Vielleicht werden sie einen guten
Einfluß auf mich haben. Ziemlich gearbeitet. —.

16.11.14.

Es wird Winter. —Gestern erhielt ich von Ficker eine freundliche
Karte. Es ist dann die Rede daß die Schiffsmannschaft von hier
wegkommt da die Schiffe über Winter nicht zu verwenden sind.
    Was wird dann mit mir werden?? Wir hören starken Geschütz-
donner von den Werken. Nicht viel gearbeitet. Abends in der Stadt.
Wieder keine Klarheit des Sehens obwohl ich ganz offenbar vor der
Lösung der tiefsten Fragen stehe daß ich mir fast die Nase daran
stoße!!! Mein Geist ist eben jetzt dafür einfach blind! Ich fühle daß
ich <u>an dem Tor</u> <u>daran</u> stehe kann es aber nicht klar genug sehen um
es öffnen zu können. Dies ist ein ungemein merkwürdiger Zustand
den ich noch nie so klar empfunden habe als jetzt. —! —!

17.11.14.

<u>Wie schwer</u> es ist sich nicht mit den Leuten zu ärgern! <u>Wie
schwer</u> es ist zu dulden. Vormittag alles Mögliche zu verrichten
gehabt & nicht zum Arbeiten gekommen. Wenn immer ich bei
der Arbeit mit den Leuten hier in Berührung komme wird mir
ihre Gemeinheit so fürchterlich daß die Wut droht in mir zu sie-
gen & auszubrechen. <u>Immer wieder</u> nehme ich mir vor ruhig zu
dulden & <u>immer</u> wieder breche ich meinen Vorsatz. Und wie dies
kommt weiß ich eigentlich selber nicht. Es ist so riesig schwer
mit Leuten zu arbeiten & dabei doch <u>nichts</u> mit ihnen zu tun zu
haben. Immer wieder muß man zu ihnen reden, sie etwas fragen, sie antworten frech & ungenügend—welcher Kraftaufwand

15.11.14.

Reading Emerson's essays* now. Perhaps they will have a good influence on me. Worked pretty hard.—.

16.11.14.

Winter is coming.— Yesterday I received a friendly card from Ficker. Now the word is that our crew will be departing from here since the ships are of no use in winter.

What will become of me then?? We can hear the loud thunder of guns from the workshop. Didn't work much. Evening in town. Again no clarity of vision, although I am evidently so close to finding the answer to the most profound questions that the solution is practically under my nose!!! Right now, my spirit is simply blind to it. I feel that I am standing in front of the gate <u>itself</u> but cannot see clearly enough to open it. It is an extremely strange state of mind that I have never before experienced as clearly as now.—!—!

17.11.14.

<u>How hard</u> it is not to get angry with these people! <u>How hard</u> to tolerate their behavior. I had all sorts of things to do this morning & did not get to my work. Whenever in the course of working I come into contact with the people here, their boorishness strikes me as so dreadful that my rage threatens to win & break out. <u>Again and again</u> I resolve to suffer it silently & <u>again</u> and again I break my resolution. And I don't know myself how this happens. It is so enormously hard to work with people & at the same time to have nothing to do with them. You have to talk to them again and again, to ask them something, they respond insolently and inadequately—

---

* Ralph Waldo Emerson (1803–1882). Wittgenstein presumably came to Emerson's transcendentalism, as in essays such as "The Over-Soul," via contemporary writings by and on Goethe.

schon, dies hinzunehmen—du brauchst aber die Antwort. Es kommt ein unklarer Befehl, etc., etc., etc. Und die Nerven sind ohnehin schon ruiniert. Da ist es schwer zu leben wenn man nicht versteht es sich ganz leicht zu machen. Nachmittag faßte mich eine schwere Depression an. Wie ein Stein liegt es auf meiner Brust. Jede Pflicht wird zur unerträglichen Bürde. Gegen Abend legte sich mein Übelbefinden. In meine Seele kehrte etwas Mut zurück. Fast nicht gearbeitet. Untertags, wie jetzt schon oft, war keine Stimmung, erst abends genügende innere Ruhe! Ob das davon kommt daß ich am Abend mich auf den Schlaf freue? – Ja, die heutige Depression war furchtbar!!! —.

18.11.14.
Starker Donner von den Werken. Es heißt daß wir in den nächsten Tagen wieder fahren sollen. Unser Kommandant kommt weg & der Leutnant Molé wieder an seine Stelle. Dies freut mich. Man hört Maschinengewehrfeuer. Den ganzen Tag heftiger Geschützdonner von den Werken. — Ziemlich viel gearbeitet. Guter Stimmung. Trage mich mit dem Plan mich versetzen zu lassen kann aber nicht mit mir in's reine darüber kommen. In meiner Arbeit ist ein Stillstand eingetreten da ich wieder einen bedeutenden Einfall brauchte um vorwärts zu kommen. ——.

19.11.14.
Es schneit. Wie jetzt oft, früh in gedrückter Stimmung. Den ganzen Vormittag für's Schiff gearbeitet. Nachmittag erwartet man den Besuch eines General's. Alles deshalb schon jetzt in Aufregung. Gegen Abend etwas gearbeitet. Wieder heftige Kämpfe um Krakau. —.

what a strain it is just to accept that—but you need their answer. An unclear order is given, etc. etc. etc. And anyway your nerves are already shot. And so it is hard to live if one doesn't understand how to make it tolerable. In the afternoon I fell into a severe depression. Like a stone it presses on my chest. Every duty turns into an unbearable burden. My depression lifted toward evening. A little strength came back into my soul. I did almost no work. During the day, as now so often, the inclination for it wasn't there, not until evening is there enough inner peace. Does this happen because in the evening I look forward to sleep?— Yes, today's depression was terrible!!!—.

18.11.14.

Strong cannon thunder from the enemy positions. It is said that in the next few days we will be sailing again. Our commander is leaving & Lieutenant Molé once again in his place. That pleases me. One can hear machine-gun fire. All day <u>heavy</u> gunfire from the fortifications. Did quite a lot of work. Good mood. Am entertaining the idea of getting myself transferred but can't come clean to myself about it. A stalemate has occurred in my work so that I would once again need a significant idea in order to move forward.——.

19.11.14.

It is snowing. As so often in the morning now, feeling quite low. Performed ship work all morning. A general's visit is awaited in the afternoon. Hence everyone already in a state of excitement. Toward evening worked a little. Again fierce battles around Kraków.—.

20.11.14.

Starke Kanonade. —. Etwas gearbeitet. Heute nacht Wache. Nachmittags beim Augenarzt weil ich beim Wachdienst unter meinen schlechten Augen leide. Werde Brillen bekommen. Meine Zukunft ist noch immer ganz ungewiß. Morgen werde ich vielleicht mit unserem Kommandanten darüber reden was mit mir geschehen soll. —

21.11.14.

Anhaltende Kanonade. Große Kälte. Fast ununterbrochener Donner von den Werken. Ziemlich gearbeitet. Aber noch immer kann ich daß eine erlösende Wort nicht aussprechen. Ich gehe rund um es herum & ganz nahe aber noch konnte ich es nicht selber erfassen!! Über meine Zukunft immer ein wenig besorgt, weil ich nicht ganz in mir ruhe! — ! —.

22.11.14.

Grimmige Kälte! Auf der Weichsel schwimmt Eis. Fortwährend Geschützdonner. Keinen rechten Einfall gehabt & recht müde daher wenig gearbeitet. Daß erlösende Wort nicht ausgesprochen. Gestern lag es mir einmal ganz auf der Zunge. Dann aber gleitet es wieder zurück —. Bin mittelmäßiger Stimmung. Ich will bald schlafen gehen. —.

22.11.14.

An dieser Stelle versuche ich wieder etwas auszudrücken, was sich nicht ausdrücken läst.

20.11.14.

Heavy cannon fire. ——. Worked a little. Watch duty tonight. To
the eye doctor's in the afternoon because I suffer from bad eye-
sight when I'm on watch. I will get glasses. My future is still quite
uncertain. Tomorrow perhaps I will have a chance to talk to our
commander as to what is supposed to happen to me.——.

21.11.14.

Persistent cannon fire. Extreme cold. Almost uninterrupted thunder from the fortifications. Worked quite a bit. But still I cannot
express <u>the one redeeming word</u>. I go round and round it & come
quite close but so far I haven't been able to grasp it!! Always a little
worried about my future because I am not quite comfortable in my
own skin——!——.

22.11.14.

Severe cold! There is ice floating on the Vistula. Constant cannon
fire. I have had no new idea & am quite tired so that I've done little
work. The redeeming word has not been articulated. Yesterday it
was on the tip of my tongue. But then it slips away again. ——. Am in
a fair mood. I want to go to sleep soon. ——.

22.11.14.*

*At this point I am again trying to express something that won't let
itself be expressed.*

———

* In this translation, the entry for November 22, 2014, is the first entry from a recto
page from *Notebooks 1914–1916*. See "A Note on the Translation and Transcription"
near the beginning of the book.

23.11.14.

Anhaltender Donner. ——. Höre gerade daß ein Telegramm gekommen ist: "Wassertransport eingestellt." Also muß sich bald ent-
scheiden was aus uns wird. —— Mein Tag vergeht jetzt in Lesen
etwas Arbeiten wobei ich natürlich immer bei mir in der Kabine
sitze. Jeden 4ten-5ten Tag Wachdienst; hie & da Kartoffelschälen,
Kohlen tragen und dergleichen. Außer dem Wachdienst habe ich
keine <u>bestimmte</u> Arbeit (der Scheinwerfer wird seit 1½ Monaten
fast nicht mehr gebraucht). Ich fühle mich daher unter den Leuten
als Faulpelz und auch in meiner vielen freien Zeit komme ich nicht
recht zur Ruhe da ich fühle ich sollte für das Schiff arbeiten aber
doch nicht weiß was. Das Beste wäre für mich eine regelmäßige
Arbeit die ich leicht vollbringen könnte & sicher. Denn eine Arbeit
der man nicht gewachsen ist ist das Ärgste. Ich werde heute trachten mit unserem Kommandanten über eine eventuelle Versetzung
zu sprechen. Dies ist geschehen & ich darf hoffen daß ich von hier
versetzt werden werde. Ziemlich gearbeitet aber immer noch ohne
Erfolg. Abends im Bad. ——.

24.11.14.

<u>Grimmige</u> Kälte! Die Weichsel ist mit treibendem Eis ganz bedeckt.
Fahren heute in den Hafen ein. Wenn ich nur schon von hier fort
wäre! Hier ist eine immerwährende Unruhe & niemand weiß was
er tun soll. Die Unteroffiziere werden immer gemeiner & einer
steckt darin den anderen an & ermutigt ihn zu immer größerer
Frechheit. Es gibt freilich auch Ausnahmen. Heute nacht Wachdienst. Kein Wachdienst. <u>Viel</u> gearbeitet. Immer wieder liegt mir
die fehlende Erkenntnis auf der Zunge. Dies ist gut. Ficker sandte
mir heute Gedichte des armen Trakl die ich für genial halte ohne
sie zu verstehen. Sie taten mir wohl. Gott mit mir!——.

23.11.14.

Continuous firestorm. —. I just heard that a telegram has arrived: "Water-transport discontinued." So there must be a decision soon as to what is to become of us.—My day now passes in reading and a little of my own work, which means that I am naturally always sitting alone in my cabin. On watch every 4th or 5th day; here and there peeling potatoes, carrying coal and so on. Except for watch duty I have no assigned work (the searchlight has no longer been needed for the past 1½ months). Among the others, I therefore feel like a slacker and even in my free time I cannot really rest since I feel I should do some work for the ship but don't know what. The best thing for me would be to have some regular job that I could dispatch easily and securely. The worst is a job one hasn't been trained for. I will try today to speak to our commander about an eventual transfer. That's done & I dare hope that I will be transferred from here. Worked pretty hard but still with no success. In the evening to the baths.—.

24.11.14.

Bitter cold! The Vistula is covered with blocks of ice. Today heading to the harbor. If only I were already away from here! There is constant turmoil here & no one knows what we're supposed to do. The noncommissioned officers become ever nastier & one man incites the next and emboldens him to be even more insolent. Of course there are exceptions. Watch duty tonight. No watch duty tonight. Worked a great deal. Again and again the missing recognition is on the tip of my tongue. This is good. Today Ficker sent me some of Trakl's poems which I consider inspiring without understanding them. They did me good. God be with me!—.

25.11.14.

Stehen seit gestern nachmittag im Hafen. Die Aborte des Schiffs sind gesperrt! Und man muß weit laufen bis zu einer halboffenen Latrine. Es ist sehr kalt. Die Lebensweise wird immer unerträglicher. Nicht viel gearbeitet. Nur fort von hier! —.

26.11.14.

Wenn man fühlt daß man bei einem Problem stockt so darf man nicht mehr darüber nachdenken sonst bleibt man daran kleben. Sondern man muß irgendwo anfangen zu denken wo man ganz gemütlich sitzen kann. Nur nicht drücken! Die harten Probleme müssen sich alle von selbst vor uns auflösen.

Starker Kanonendonner.

Was ich auch tue, die Probleme ballen sich wie Gewitterwolken zusammen und ich bin nicht im Stande einen dauernd befriedigenden Standpunkt ihnen gegenüber einzunehmen. Sehr viel gearbeitet aber ohne die Lage irgendwie klären zu können. Vielmehr wo ich immer denke überall treffe ich Fragen die ich nicht beantworten kann. Heute war es mir als sei es nun mit meiner Fruchtbarkeit zu Ende. Der ganze Gegenstand schien wieder in die Ferne zu rücken. Und freilich: meine 3–4 Monate sind um. Und leider ohne ein wirklich großes Resultat! Aber wir werden ja sehen. —Es heißt jetzt daß wir Winterquartiere beziehen sollen und wenn dies geschieht werde ich vielleicht mit allen Leuten zusammen schlafen müssen; was Gott verhüte!! —

Möchte in jedem Fall die Geistesgegenwart nicht verlieren! Gott mit mir.— —.

27.11.14.

Heute Wache. —.

25.11.14.

Moored since yesterday afternoon in the harbor. The ship's toilets are locked! And you have to run far to find a half-open latrine. It is very cold. This way of life is becoming more and more unbearable. Didn't work much. Only to get out of here!——.

26.11.14.

When you feel that a problem is bogging you down, you must not think about it any more, otherwise it sticks in your mind. Rather, you must somehow begin your thinking in an area where you feel at home. Only don't force things! The difficult problems must all solve themselves on their own.

   Loud cannon thunder.

Whatever I do, the problems mount up like gathering thunder-clouds and I am in no condition to assess them from a satisfactory perspective. Worked very hard but somehow without being able to clear up the difficulty. On the contrary, precisely when it comes to the things I am always thinking about, I meet questions every-where that I can't answer. Today I felt that the fertility of my mind may have dried up. The whole topic of my work seemed to move off into the distance. And indeed: my 3–4 months are over. Sadly, without any really major result. But we shall see.—The word is now that we are to move into winter quarters and if that happens I may have to share sleeping quarters with the other men; God forbid!!—

I hope in any case not to lose my presence of mind! God be with me! —— —.

27.11.14.

Watch duty today. —.

28.11.14.

Gestern sehr viel gearbeitet. Von gestern mittag bis heute mittag im Wachzimmer mit 7 Leuten & am Posten. Fühlte mich—besonders heute sehr unglücklich. Betreibe mit allen Mitteln meine Versetzung. Ich glaube daß ich in der Umgebung dieser rohen & gemeinen Menschen die durch keine Gefahr gezähmt sind elend umkommen <u>muß</u> wenn nicht ein Wunder für mich geschieht das mir viel mehr Kraft & Weisheit gibt als ich jetzt habe! Ja, ein <u>Wunder</u> müßte für mich geschehen wenn ich es überleben soll! Bin in Angst wegen meiner Zukunft. Wenig gearbeitet. Ein Wunder! Ein Wunder! —.

29.11.14.

Ziemlich viel gearbeitet. —.

30.11.14.

Früh am Korpskommando. Mit unserem Kommandanten wegen mir gesprochen: Wenn ich versetzt werde so muß ich zurück zum Kader kommen. Im Falle wir Winterquartiere beziehen wird er dafür sorgen daß ich ein eigenes Zimmer kriege. In der nächsten Zeit aber soll der Scheinwerfer wieder gebraucht werden & ich solle doch daher hier bleiben. — Jetzt abends wie ich aus der Stadt komme ist hier großer Lärm weil ein Schiff von hier wegfahren soll. Es ist auch die Rede davon daß der Scheinwerfer mitkommt. —. Dies wäre mir recht unangenehm. So können unsere Pläne jeden Augenblick durchkreuzt werden & ich muß einen anderen Halt haben um <u>doch</u> leben zu können. — War heute nachmittag beim Kader & sprach mit einem Feuerwerker darüber ob es nicht möglich wäre daß ich in die Ballonabteilung käme. Er sagte ich

28.11.14.

Yesterday worked very hard. From yesterday noon till today noon in the guardroom with 7 men & on duty. I felt—especially today—very unlucky. I am trying by all possible means to get my transfer. I fear that in the company of these crude and mean-spirited men, whom no danger can tame, I <u>must</u> come to a miserable end unless a miracle takes place that gives me much more power and wisdom than I have now! Yes, a <u>miracle</u> must happen to me if I am to survive this! I am anxious about my future. Worked very little. A miracle! A miracle!—.

29.11.14.

Worked pretty hard.—.

30.11.14.

To command headquarters in the morning. Talked to our commander about my situation. If I am to be transferred, I must first go back to my squadron. In case we occupy winter quarters, he will see to it that I get my own room. In the immediate future, however, they will need the searchlight again & I am therefore to stay here.— As I was coming back from town this evening, there was a huge uproar because a ship is supposed to depart from here. There is also talk of taking the searchlight along.—. That would be very unpleasant for me. So I see that our plans can fall through at any moment & I must develop a different attitude in order to live <u>despite it all</u>.— Went to the squadron command this afternoon & spoke to a master-sergeant about the possibility of my being transferred to the balloon division. He said I should speak with a master-sergeant

solle hierüber mit einem Feuerwerker Vlcek dieser Abteilung sprechen. Dies werde ich hoffentlich tun können! — Nicht viel gearbeitet aber nicht ohne Anregung. Wieder etwas sinnlich.

Nur dem eigenen Geist leben! und alles Gott überlassen! —.

1.12.14.

Also schon Dezember! und noch immer keine Rede von Frieden! Heute nacht heftiger Geschützdonner, man hörte die Geschosse sausen. —Gestern Abend ist ein Schiff die Weichsel hinunter gefahren und jeden Tag hat eine andere Besatzung darauf Wache z.B. morgen wir! Wie wird es mir ergehen?! Mit diesen Kameraden & diesen Vorgesetzten! — —. Nachmittag den Feuerwerker Vlcek suchen gegangen, nicht gefunden. Wurde an die Artilleriestabsabteilung gewiesen. Werde wohl übermorgen nach der Wache dorthin gehen. Sehr wenig gearbeitet. Der Geist beschütze mich was immer geschehe! —.

2.12.14.

Heute mittag gehen wir auf Wache. Gott sei Dank geht unser Kommandant mit so daß wenigstens <u>ein</u> anständiger Mensch dabei ist. Nachts furchtbarer Donner von den Werken. Und jetzt um 8 Uhr früh fängt er wieder an. Heute nacht müssen wir im Freien schlafen. Ich werde wohl nicht zum Arbeiten kommen; nur Gott nicht vergessen. ——.

3.12.14

Nichts gearbeitet aber viel erlebt, bin aber jetzt zu müde es einzutragen. —

from that division named Vlcek. I hope to be able to do this!——.
Haven't done much work but am eager to get to it. Feeling sexually
aroused again.

Only to be true to one's own spirit! And leave everything to
God!——.

1.12.14.

Already December! And still no talk of peace!* Today after strong
rifle fire one could hear the bullets zooming.——. Yesterday evening
a ship came down the Vistula and every day a different crew has to
be on watch for it, for example, tomorrow, our turn! How will I get
through it?! With these "comrades" & these superiors!———. Went
to look for Sergeant Vlcek in the afternoon, but couldn't find him.
I was directed to the artillery division. Will probably go over there
after the watch the day after tomorrow. Worked very little. May the
spirit protect me whatever happens!——.

2.12.14.

We are going on watch duty at noon today. Thank God our commander is going with us so that at least there will be <u>one</u> decent
man there. At night terrible firestorm from the fortifications. It's
now 8 a.m. and beginning again. Tonight we have to sleep out in
the open. I will probably not get to work; only let me not forget God.
— —.

3.12.14.

Didn't work but experienced a great deal, but I'm too tired to write
about it right now.——

---

* By December 1914, it was becoming obvious to both sides that the war, originally
projected to last weeks and at most a few months, was going to last a long time.

4.12.14.

Vorgestern auf der Wacht ereignete sich nichts Besonderes außer daß ich einmal laufend zu Boden fiel und noch heute hinken muß. Von allen Seiten heftigster Kanonendonner. Gewehrfeuer, Brände etc. Gestern abend auf dem Festungskommando wegen meiner Angelegenheit. Ein Oberleutnant, als er hörte, daß ich Mathematik studient hatte sagte ich solle zu ihm (in eine Fabrik) kommen. Er scheint <u>sehr</u> nett zu sein. Ich willigte ein und wurde heute von diesen Schiff abkommandiert. Ich habe viel Hoffnung.—. Geschützdonner in nächster Nähe. Nachmittag in der Stadt. Wenig gearbeitet. War den ganzen Tag über etwas müde da ich auch in der letzten Nacht sehr wenig geschlafen habe. Früh zu Bett!—.

5.12.14.

Morgen oder übermorgen gehe ich von hier weg. Wo ich wohnen werde ist noch nicht bestimmt. In keinem Fall will ich von solchen Sachen abhängen. Nicht viel gearbeitet; doch stehe ich nicht still. Denke <u>viel</u> an den <u>lieben</u> David! Gott behüte ihn! und mich!

6.12.14.

Nachts feuerten die Kanonen ganz in der Nähe daß das Schiff zitterte. Viel gearbeitet & mit Erfolg. Noch nicht erfahren wann ich von dem Schiff wegkomme. Morgen hat dieses Schiff wieder Feldwache & wenn ich nicht morgen abberufen werde so werde ich mitgehen müssen was mir sehr unangenehm ist weil mein Bein noch immer nicht von dem Sturz geheilt ist. Es regnet & die Lehmwege hier sind furchtbar schlecht zu gehen. Der Geist beschütze mich!.——

4.12.14.

On the watch day before yesterday nothing unusual happened except that, while running, I slipped and fell to the floor and am still limping. The heaviest cannon fire, rifle fire, bombs, etc. from all sides. Went to the command headquarters yesterday about my case. A First Lieutenant, who had heard that I had studied mathematics, said I should work with him (in a factory). He seems to be very nice. I agreed to go and today I was discharged from this ship. I have high hopes.——. Gunfire very close by. Afternoon in town. Worked very little. I was a little tired all day because I slept very little last night. Early to bed! ——.

5.12.14

I am leaving here tomorrow or the day after tomorrow. Where I will live is not yet decided. In any case, I will not let myself depend on such practical issues. Didn't work much; but am not just at a standstill. I think a great deal about dear David! God protect him! And me!

6.12.14.

Last night the cannon fire was so close that the ship shook. Worked hard & successfully. I have not yet heard when I am to leave the ship. Tomorrow this ship has watch duty once again & if I am not called away I will have to participate, which is very annoying because my leg has still not healed from the fall. It is raining & the clay paths here are terribly slippery. May the spirit protect me!.——

7.12.14.

Mein Bein schlechter geworden. Werde wohl nicht mit auf Wache gehen. Meine Übersiedelung betreffend ist noch kein Befehl gekommen. Starker Donner in der Nähe. —. Erfahre soeben daß ich morgen von hier abgehen werde. Kann meines Fußes wegen nicht auf Wache gehen. Nicht viel gearbeitet. Mit unserem Kommandanten gesprochen, er war sehr nett. Bin müde. Alles in Gottes Hand.

8.12.14.

Vormittag bei der "Marodenvisite" wegen meines Fußes: Muskelzerrung. Nicht viel gearbeitet. Nietzsche Band 8 gekauft & darin gelesen. Bin stark berührt von seiner Feindschaft gegen das Christentum. Denn auch in seinen Schriften ist etwas Wahrheit enthalten. Gewiß, das Christentum ist der einzige <u>sichere</u> Weg zum Glück; aber wie wenn einer dieses Glück verschmähte?! Könnte es nicht besser sein, unglücklich im hoffnungslosen Kampf gegen die äußere Welt zu Grunde zu gehen? Aber ein solches Leben ist sinnlos. Aber warum nicht ein sinnloses Leben führen? Ist es unwürdig? — Wie verträgt es sich mit dem streng solipsistischen Standpunkt? Was muß ich aber tun daß mein Leben mir nicht verloren geht? Ich muß mir seiner immer — des Geistes immer — bewußt sein. —.

9.12.14.

Vormittag am Korpskommando & meinen Verpflegszettel geholt. Nicht gearbeitet. Sehr viel erlebt aber zu müde es einzutragen.—.

7.12.14.

My leg has gotten worse. I probably won't go on watch duty with the others. No order has yet been given with regard to my move. Heavy thunder close by.— Have just learned that I will be leaving here tomorrow. Can't go on watch because of my foot. Didn't work much. I spoke to our commander, who was very nice. I'm tired. Everything is in God's hands.

8.12.14.

To the "Sick-Call Clinic" in the morning because of my foot: muscle strain. Didn't work much. Bought Nietzsche Volume 8 & read in it.* I am deeply moved by his hostility to Christianity. For there is always some truth in his writings. Certainly, Christianity is the only <u>sure</u> path to happiness; but how would it be if someone disdained such happiness? Might it not be better for the unhappy one, in his hopeless struggle against the external world, to go under? But such a life makes no sense. But why not live a life that makes no sense? Is it unworthy? — How can it be reconciled with the strictly solipsistic position? But what must I do so that my life will not be lost? I must always—be conscious always—of the spirit. —.

9.12.14.

To the army command corps in the morning to get my handicap permit. Did no work. Experienced a great deal but too tired to set it down now.

---

* Friedrich Nietzsche (1844–1900) was a central influence on the young Wittgenstein. Volume 8 of the Leipzig edition, referred to here, contains, among other writings "The Antichrist," which was the first book of the intended *The Will to Power*. The volume also contains "The Case of Wagner," "Götzen-Dämmerung," "Nietzsche contra Wagner," and Nietzsche's poems.

10.12.14.

Gestern nachmittag in die Kanzlei zu meinem neuen Chef. Mußte lange auf ihn warten. Endlich kam er & gab mir sofort eine Arbeit ich mußte eine Liste von Motorwägen in einer Kaserne hier zusammenstellen. Zugleich lud er mich für 8 Uhr abends zu sich in die Wohnung ein: ein Hauptmann sei dort dem er von mir erzählt habe & der mich sehen möchte. Kam zu ihm & fand 4 Offiziere bei ihm mit denen ich nachtmahlte. Der Hauptmann ist ein unendlich sympathischer Mann (auch alle anderen waren riesig liebenswürdig). Wir sprachen bis 10½ & schieden ungemein herzlich. — Heute früh Wohnung gesucht & gefunden. Von 10 bis abends 5 im Bureau, dann meine Sachen vom Schiff hierher in die neue Wohnung getragen: ein ganz nettes nicht kleines Zimmer.

Seit 4 Monaten zum ersten Mal allein in einem wirklichen Zimmer!! Ich genieße diesen Luxus: Nicht zum Arbeiten gekommen. Aber es wird jetzt schon werden. Bin sehr müde da ich sehr viel herum gerannt bin. Welche Gnade wieder in einem Bett schlafen zu dürfen! Welche Gnade der Tatsache. — —.

11.12.14.

Vormittag in der Kanzlei & geschrieben. Nicht zum Arbeiten gekommen. Ganzen Tag Kanzlei. Oberleutnant außerordentlich lieb. Nicht zum Arbeiten gekommen.

12.12.14.

Ein wenig gearbeitet. War den ganzen Tag in der Kanzlei hatte aber nicht viel zu tun. Hoffe morgen mehr zu arbeiten. Gebadet. —.

13.12.14.

Ganzen Tag Kanzlei. Meine Gedanken sind lahm. Ich habe Muskelschmerzen im Bein & es ist als ob auch mein Gehirn hinkte. Doch

10.12.14.

Went to the office to see my new commander yesterday afternoon; I had to wait for him for a long time. Finally he came & immediately gave me a job: to assemble a list of the motor cars found in one barracks. At the same time he invited me to come to his quarters at 8 p.m.: a captain would be there, to whom the commander had mentioned me & who would like to meet me. I went there & found 4 officers with whom I dined. The captain is a remarkably appealing man (the others were also extremely gracious). We talked till half past ten & parted very cordially.———This morning I looked for & found a flat. I was at the office from 10 to 5 p.m., then I brought my things from the ship here to the new flat: quite a nice little room, not too small.

For the first time in 4 months I have a real room of my own!! I am <u>enjoying</u> this luxury: I didn't get to do any work. But now I will get there. I am <u>very</u> tired because I had to run around a lot. What a blessing to be able to sleep in a bed again! What a blessed turn of events. — —.

11.12.14.

In the morning in the office & wrote orders. Didn't get to my own work. All day at the office. The first lieutenant is exceptionally nice. Didn't get to my work.

12.12.14.

Worked a little. Was in the office all day but not much to do. Hope to be able to work tomorrow. Bathed. — .

13.12.14.

At the office all day. <u>My thoughts are lame</u>. I have muscle aches in my leg & it's as if my mind were limping too. But I did a little work.

etwas gearbeitet. Noch immer keine Antwort von David! Ob er meinen Brief erhalten hat? Ob er den Krieg persönlicher auffaßt als ich?! — Lebe nur der Geist! Er ist der sichere Hafen geschützt abseits vom trostlosen unendlichen grauen Meer des Geschehens. —.

14.12.14.

Ganzen Tag Kanzlei. Nicht gearbeitet. Es wird aber schon wieder werden! Liebe Sendung von der Jolles. —.

15.12.14.

Ganzen Tag Kanzlei. Etwas gearbeitet. Aber meine Gedanken sind so wie in der Eisenbahn oder auf dem Schiff wo man auch in der selben Weise schwerfällig denkt.

16.12.14.

Ganzen Tag Kanzelei. Hörte daß wir wahrscheinlich bald nach Lodz über siedeln! Etwas gearbeitet aber ohne wirklichen Animo.

17.12.14.

Ganzen Tag Kanzlei. Nicht gearbeitet. Mich viel geärgert. — Sehr wenig freie Zeit. —.

18.12.14.

Wie gewöhnlich. Nicht gearbeitet.

19.12.14.

Ein wenig gearbeitet. —.

Still no answer from David! I wonder if he got my letter? And if he takes the war more personally than I do?!—— Only let the spirit live! He is the safe haven, protected from the desolate, boundless gray seas of happenings.—.

14.12.14.
At the office all day. Did no work. But it will come back! Kind message from Frau Jolles.—.

15.12.14.
At the office all day. Worked a little. But my thoughts are like those one has on a train or a ship where one can think only with difficulty.

16.12.14.
All day at the office. I heard that we will probably soon move to Lodz! Worked a bit but without any real inclination.

17.12.14.
At the office all day. Didn't work. Was muchly irritated.—Very little free time.—.

18.12.14.
As usual. Did no work.

19.12.14
Worked a little.—.

20.12.14.

Ein wenig gearbeitet. Bis fast 5 in der Kanzlei dann in die Stadt. Das angenehme Gefühl eines kleinen kalten Laufens den Rücken hinunter wenn man sich bei guter Stimmung seiner Einsamkeit bewußt wird. —.

21.12.14.

Brief von David!! Ich habe ihn geküßt. Antwortete gleich. Ein wenig gearbeitet.—.

22.12.14.

Nicht gearbeitet. Bis 6 Kanzlei.—. Ganz wenig gearbeitet. Abends gebadet.—

24.12.14.

Wurde heute zu meiner größten Überraschung zum Militärbeam-ten—ohne Sterne— befördert. Nicht gearbeitet. —.

25.12.14.

In der Offiziersmesse zu Mittag gegessen. Etwas gearbeitet.

26.12.14.

Fast nicht gearbeitet. Lernte nachmittag einen jungen Menschen kennen der in Lemberg Hochschüler war & jetzt hier Chauffeur ist. Abends mit ihm im Kaffeehaus & mich gut unterhalten. —.

20.12.14.

Worked a little. At the office till almost 5 and then in the city. The pleasant feeling of a little cold stream running down one's back when one is in the mood to appreciate one's solitude. —.

21.12.14.

A letter from David!! I kissed it. Answered right away. Worked a little. —.

22.12.14.

Did no work. Until 6 at office.—. Worked very little. In the evening, went to the baths.—

24.12.14.

Today to my greatest surprise promoted to *Militärbeamter**—without decoration— Did no work. —.

25.12.14.

Ate dinner in the officers' mess. Worked a little.

26.12.14.

Did almost no work. In the afternoon made the acquaintance of a young man who was a university student in Lemberg & is now a driver here. In the evening went to café with him and had a good time.—.

---

* Designated a clerk, not given a rank but on special assignment as assistant to the *Oberleutnant.*

27.12.14.

Bis 9½ p.m. Kanzlei. Nicht gearbeitet. Bin zum Adjutanten des Oberleutnant Gürth ernannt. ———.

28.12.14.

Bis 10 p.m. Kanzlei. Nicht gearbeitet. <u>Sehr</u> <u>viel zu tun.</u> ——.

29.12.14.

Ein klein wenig gearbeitet. Sonst viel zu tun. Abends Bad.

30.12.14.

Nicht gearbeitet. Nur sich nicht verlieren. ———.

2.1.15.

Vorgestern nachmittag erfuhr ich plötzlich daß ich mit meinem Kommandanten gleich nach Wien fahren solle. Gestern früh kamen wir hier in Wien an. Begreiflich höchste Überraschung & Freude der Mama. etc. Gestern nichts gearbeitet sondern lediglich mich meiner Familie gewidmet. Heute vormittag Besorgungen. Jetzt zu Mittag erwarte ich Gürth mit dem ich Dienstliches zu erledigen habe. Notieren will ich mir daß mein moralischer Stand jetzt viel tiefer ist als etwa zu Ostern.

3.1.15.

Gestern nachmittag mit Gürth in Klosterneuburg. Dann mit Mama zuhause.

27.12.14.

At the office till 9:30 p.m. Didn't work. Have been named adjutant to First Lieutenant Gürth. ——.

28.12.14.

At the office till 10 p.m. Didn't work. <u>Very much to do.</u> —.

29.12.14.

Worked a little bit. Much other business to do. In the evening, the baths.

30.12.14.

Did no work. Only not to lose oneself.——.

2.1.15.

I was suddenly informed, day before yesterday afternoon, that I would be going to Vienna with my commander. We arrived here in Vienna yesterday morning. Naturally the greatest surprise and pleasure for Mama. etc. Last night did not work but devoted myself entirely to my family. Errands this morning. I am waiting now at noon for Gürth with whom I have to settle some business. Let me note here that my moral standing is now much lower than it was at Easter.

3.1.15.

With Gürth in Klosterneuburg* yesterday afternoon. Then at home with Mama.

---

* Small town with famous abbey about ten miles from Vienna.

6.1.15.

Wien. Morgen Rückfahrt. Vorvorgestern & vorgestern bei Labor. Gestern mit Gürth in Wienerneustadt am Rückweg in Mödling mit einem Hauptmann Roth gespeist der mir unendlich unsympathisch war. Fuhr deshalb gleich nach Tisch allein mit der Bahn nach Wien.

10.1.15.

Heute spät abends in Krakau angekommen. Bin müde!
Hatte viele sehr gemütliche Stunden mit Gürth. Bin auf mein zukünftiges Leben sehr neugierig. —.

11.1.15.

Karte von Frege erhalten! Ein wenig gearbeitet.

12.1.15.

Etwas gearbeitet. —.

13.1.15.

Etwas gearbeitet. Arbeite noch nicht mit großem Animo. Meine Gedanken sind müde. Ich sehe die Sachen nicht frisch sondern alltäglich, ohne Leben. Es ist als ob eine Flamme erloschen wäre & ich muß warten bis sie von selbst wieder zu brennen anfängt. Mein Geist aber ist rege: Ich denke . . . —.

14.1.15.

Ein wenig gearbeitet; noch nicht gut. Denke sehr oft an David. Und lange nach einem Brief von ihm.

6.1.15.

Vienna. The return trip tomorrow. At Labor's* the past two days. Then yesterday with Gürth to Wienerneustadt, on the trip back dined in Mödling with a Captain Roth whom I found terribly unappealing. Accordingly, right after dinner, I took the train back to Vienna all by myself.

10.1.15.

Arrived in Kraków late in the evening. I am tired!
Had many very pleasant hours with Gürth. Am very curious about my future life.—.

11.1.15.

Received a card from Frege! Worked a little.

12.1.15.

Worked a little. —.

13.1.15.

Worked a little. Not yet working with much gusto. My thoughts are tired. I don't see things with new eyes but from a banal perspective, lifelessly. It is as if a flame had been extinguished & I must wait till it begins to burn again of its own accord. My spirit however is active: I am thinking . . . —.

14.1.15.

Worked a little. Not yet any good. Think very often about David. And I long for a letter from him.

---

* Josef Labor (1842–1924), composer, organist, and music teacher, blind from birth, who was a protegé of the Wittgenstein family, frequent performer at their house, and also music teacher to their children.

15.1.15.

Etwas gearbeitet; mit größerem Animo. Abends gebadet.

16.1.15.

Mehr gearbeitet & mit Animo. Habe jetzt sehr wenig fürs Detachement zu tun was mir sehr angenehm ist. Noch keine Nachricht von David. In den letzten Wochen sinnlicher. ———.

17.1.15.

Wieder gearbeitet.——.

18.1.15.

Fast nichts gearbeitet. Fühlte mich ganz matt & ohne jedes Animo. Es wird aber wohl anders werden. ——. ———.

19.1.15.

Sehr wenig gearbeitet. In dieser Beziehung ganz tot. Nur sich zu nichts zwingen!!! Wann werde ich eine Nachricht von David erhalten?! ——.

20.1.15.

Nicht gearbeitet; aber diese Ruhe ist wie der erquickende Schlaf.

20.1.15.

… Daß erlösende Wort——?

21.1.15.

Etwas gearbeitet. Brief an David abgeschickt. Ging mit ihm direkt zum Zensor an der hiesigen Hauptpost der ein sehr netter Mensch ist.

15.1.15.
Did a little work; with greater gusto. In the evening, to the baths.

16.1.15.
Did more work & with gusto. Now have very little to do for the unit, which is very pleasant for me. No news yet from David. In the last few weeks more often sexually aroused. ———.

17.1.15.
Worked again.—.

18.1.15.
Did almost no work. Felt quite dull and lacking any energy. But things will surely change. —. ———.

19.1.15.
Worked very little. In this respect, I feel quite dead. But one must not to force oneself!!! When will I receive news from David?!—.

20.1.15.
Did no work; but this rest period is like a refreshing sleep.

20.1.15.
. . . The redeeming word—?

21.1.15.
Worked a little. Sent David a letter. Took it directly to the local post office to the censor, who is a very nice man.

22.1.15.

Gearbeitet.

23.1.15.

Etwas gearbeitet. Komme jetzt durch meine unausgesprochene Stellung in Schwierigkeiten. Nur sich selbst besitzen! —.

24.1.15.

Etwas gearbeitet——.

25.1.15.

Brief von Keynes! Nicht sehr lieb. In den letzten Tagen sehr sinn-lich. — Ohne Erfolg gearbeitet. Ich bin ganz im Dunkeln darüber wie meine Arbeit weiter gehen wird. <u>Nur</u> durch Wunder kann sie gelingen. Nur dadurch indem <u>von außerhalb mir</u> der Schleier von meinen Augen weggenommen wird. Ich muß mich <u>ganz</u> in mein Schicksal ergeben. Wie es über mich verhängt ist so wird es wer-den. Ich lebe in der Hand des Schicksals. (Nur nicht klein werden.) Und so kann ich nicht klein werden. —.

26.1.15.

Liebe Karte von Arne erhalten. Etwas—aber erfolglos—gearbeitet.

22.1.15.

Worked.

23.1.15.

Worked a little. I am now getting into trouble for my unspoken position. Only to be in command of oneself! — .

24.1.15.

Worked a little.———.

25.1.15.

Letter from Keynes!! Not very warm.* Feeling strong sexual desire in the last few days.— Worked without success. I am quite in the dark as to what direction my work will take. <u>Only</u> through a miracle can it succeed. Only if the veil over my eyes fall <u>of its own accord</u>. I have to submit entirely to my fate. Whatever is imposed on me, will be. I live in the hands of fate. (Only don't become petty.) And so I cannot become petty.—.

26.1.15.

Received lovely card from Arne.** Did a little—but without success—work.

---

* Keynes's letter was more ironic than affectionate. "I hope," he writes, "you have been safely taken prisoner by now. Russell and I have given up philosophy for the present—I to give my services to govt. for financial business, he to agitate for peace" (see Monk, *Ludwig Wittgenstein*, 124).

** Arne Bolstad, a teenage village boy Wittgenstein befriended during his first stay in Skjolden, Norway, in 1913. In 1919, Wittgenstein, assuming he would never return to Skjolden, deeded his spartan cottage in the mountains to Bolstad. But he was to change his mind about wanting it and returned to the Skjolden cottage in 1921, 1936–1937, and 1950, although he was no longer the official owner. After Wittgenstein's death in 1951, Bolstad had the cottage dismantled and re-erected as a modest home inside the village. The hut, recently restored as a Wittgenstein memorial, reopened for view in 2019.

27.1.15.

Nicht gearbeitet. Abends mit vielen Offizieren im Kaffee. Die meisten benahmen sich wie Schweine. Selbst ich trank ein ganz klein wenig mehr als nötig.

28.1.15.

Nicht gearbeitet was mir sehr gesund ist—nämlich der Arbeit. Sehr sinnlich was merkwürdig ist weil ich jetzt nicht wenig Bewegung mache. Schlafe nicht gut.

29.1.15.

Fast nicht gearbeitet.

30.1.15.

Nicht gearbeitet. Habe mich viel über meine äußere Stellung aufregen müssen & werde in dieser Sache wahrscheinlich bald einen entscheidenden Schritt tun. ————.

31.1.15.

Nicht gearbeitet. ——.

1.2.15.

Nicht gearbeitet. Zu Mittag in der Offiziersmesse des Hauptmannes Scholz wo es sehr gemütlich war. —.

2.2.15.

Ein klein wenig gearbeitet. —

3.2.15.

Nicht gearbeitet. Keine Ideen. Soll jetzt die Aufsicht über unsere Schmiede übernehmen. Wie wird das gehen? Möge der Geist mir beistehen! Es wird sehr schwierig werden aber: nur Mut! —.——.

27.1.15.

Did no work. Spent the evening with many officers in the café. Most of them behaved like pigs. Even I drank a little more than I should have.

28.1.15.

Did no work which is very good for me—it will advance the work later. Strong sexual desire which is odd because now I am getting more than a little exercise. Don't sleep well.

29.1.15.

Did almost no work.

30.1.15.

Did no work. I have been too upset about my external situation & will probably have to take a decisive step in this matter soon.————.

31.1.15.

Did no work ——.

1.2.15.

Did no work. Lunch in the officers' dining room of Captain Scholz, where it was very pleasant.—.

2.2.15.

Worked a little bit.—.

3.2.15.

Did no work. No ideas. I am now supposed to take over the supervision of our munitions factory. How will that go? May the spirit stand by me! It will be very difficult but: courage! —.——.

5.2.15.

Nicht gearbeitet. Bin jetzt viel in der Schmiede. —.

6.2.15.

Lieben Brief von David (vom 14.1.).

7.2.15.

Nicht gearbeitet. —!—.

8.2.15.

Von Ficker ein nachgelassenes Werk Trakls erhalten. Wahrscheinlich sehr gut. — Sinnlich. Habe jetzt gar keine Handhabe für
meine Arbeit. — ——.

9.2.15.

Nicht gearbeitet. — ——.

10.2.15.

Nicht gearbeitet. Netten Brief von Ficker. Widmung von Rilke.
Könnte ich nur schon wieder arbeiten!!! Alles andere würde sich finden. Wann wird mir wieder etwas einfallen??! Alles das liegt in Gottes Hand. Wünsche nur und hoffe! Dann verlierst du keine Zeit——.

11.2.15.

Nicht gearbeitet. — Stehe jetzt mit einem der Offiziere—dem
Kadetten Adam—auf sehr gespannten Fuße. Es ist möglich daß es

5.2.15.

Did no work. Now spending much time at the factory. —.

6.2.15.

Sweet letter from David (from 14.1.)

7.2.15.

Did no work. —!—.

8.2.15.

Received from Ficker a posthumous book of Trakl's poems. Probably very good.— Feeling sexually aroused. I now have no handle on my work. — ——.

9.2.15.

Did no work. — ——.

10.2.15.

Did no work. Nice letter from Ficker. Sent me Rilke's dedication.*
If only I could work again!!! Everything else would fall into place.
When will I have an idea again??! All of this lies in God's hands.
You can only wish and hope! Then you lose no time.——.

11.2.15.

Did no work.—My relationship with one of the officers—Cadet Adam—is now very tense. It is possible that it may come to a duel

---

* On February 13, 1915, Wittgenstein wrote Ficker to thank him for the testimonials from the various artists and poets who had received his financial aid: see Editor's Note earlier. Wittgenstein found most of the letters cloying and dull but singled out Rilke's: "Rilke's letter to you touched and pleased me enormously. The affection of any superior human being is a support in the unsteady balance of my life. I am quite unworthy of this wonderful present" (Wittgenstein, *Briefe*, 70).

zwischen uns zu einem Duell kommt. Lebe deswegen immer noch gut & nach deinem Gewissen. Der Geist sei mit mir! Jetzt und in jeder Zukunft! —— —.

13.2.15.

Nicht gearbeitet. Der Geist sei mit mir. ——.

15.2.15.

Gestern etwas gearbeitet. Es vergeht ja jetzt kein Tag an dem ich nicht einmal wenn auch nur flüchtig an die Logik denke & dies ist ein gutes Zeichen. Ich ahne alles Mögliche! —Gestern abend bei Hauptmann Scholz wo musiziert wurde (bis 12 a.m.). Sehr gemütlich.

17.2.15.

Gestern & heute etwas gearbeitet. Meine Stellung im Detachement ist jetzt durchaus unbefriedigend, es wird etwas geschehen müssen. — Ich muß mich viel ärgern & kränken und meine innere Kraft vergeuden. Bin wieder sehr sinnlich & onaniere fast jeden Tag: So geht es nicht weiter. —

18.2.15.

Fast nicht gearbeitet. Viel über meine Lage nachgedacht. Ich bin auf meine Zukunft in jeder Hinsicht neugierig. —.

19.2.15.

Neuerliche Unannehmlichkeiten in der Fabrik. Langes Gespräch mit meinem Kommandanten das aber zu nichts Rechtem geführt hat. Fast nicht gearbeitet. Diese Unannehmlichkeiten stören mich im Denken. Das muß anders werden. —. —.

between us. All the more important therefore to live a good life & follow your conscience. The spirit be with me! Now and in whatever the future may bring!——.

13.2.15.
Did no work. The spirit be with me.——.

15.2.15.
Worked a bit yesterday. Not a day goes by now that I don't think, even if only in passing, about logic & that is a good sign. I anticipate all sorts of things! — Last night, visited Captain Scholz's quarters where there was music making (till 12 a.m.). Very pleasant.

17.2.15.
Worked a little yesterday & today. My position in the workshop is now highly unsatisfactory; something will have to happen.——. I have to endure much irritation & insult and I am squandering my inner strength. I am having strong sexual feelings again and masturbate almost every day: it cannot go on like this——.

18.2.15.
Did almost no work. Thought a great deal about my situation. I am in every respect curious about my future. —.

19.2.15.
Recent inconveniences at the factory. Long conversation with my commander but it didn't lead to anything substantial. Did almost no work. These inconveniences disturb my thinking. It must change.——.——.

20.2.15

Feiger Gedanken bängliches Schwanken, ängstliches Zagen, weibliches Klagen, wendet kein Elend, <u>macht dich nicht frei</u>! Nicht gearbeitet. Viel gedacht. ———.

21.2.15.

Nicht gearbeitet. Besserer Stimmung. Sinnlich. Könnte ich nur schon wieder arbeiten!!!! —!—.

22.2.15.

Nicht gearbeitet. Heute nacht riesig viel und lebhaft aber nicht schlecht geträumt. Viel Unannehmlichkeiten mit der Mannschaft. Ärger & Aufregung; Selbstvorwürfe etc. etc. —,—.

23.2.15.

Nicht gearbeitet. Meine Schwierigkeiten noch immer nicht geregelt. ——.

26.2.15.

Nicht gearbeitet! Werde ich je wieder arbeiten?!? Trüber Stimmung. Keine Nachricht von David. Bin ganz verlassen. Denke an Selbstmord. Werde ich je wieder arbeiten??! — ——.

27.2.15

Nicht gearbeitet. Trübe Stimmung. Sehr sinnlich. Fühle mich vereinsamt. Das Ziel meiner Arbeit scheint mir mehr denn je in unabsehbare Ferne gerückt! Der siegesgewisse und kühn hoffende Mut fehlt mir. Es ist mir als sollte ich nie mehr eine große Entdeckung

20.2.15.

"Cowardly thinking, hesitant shrinking, anxious delaying, female complaining, cannot cure your misery, <u>cannot make you free!</u>"* Did no work. Thought a great deal.——.

21.2.15.

Did no work. Better mood. Feeling desirous. If only I could already work again!!!!—!—.

22.2.15.

Did no work. Countless vivid but not unpleasant dreams last night. Many difficulties with the crew. Anger & anxiety; self-reproaches etc. etc.——,—.

23.2.15.

Did no work. My difficulties have still not been resolved.——.

26.2.15.

Did no work. Will I ever work again?!? Dark mood. No news from David. I am entirely deserted. Contemplating suicide. Will I ever work again ??!———.

27.2.15.

Did no work. Dark mood. Strong sexual desire. Feeling lonely. More than ever, the goal of my work seems to me to have been moved into an unpredictable future. I have lost all hope and confidence in my power to succeed. It is as if I will never again make a big dis-

---

* Citation from Goethe's "Lila": "Von allen guten Geistern verlassen" ("Abandoned by all good spirits").

machen schon lang war ich nicht so von allen guten Geistern verlassen wie jetzt. Verliere nur nicht dich selbst!! —.—.

28.2.15. / 1.3.15.
Nicht gearbeitet. Keine Nachricht von David. Unentschiedener und
Wechselnder Stimmung.

2.3.15. / 3.3.15.
Nicht gearbeitet. Gestern abend einen momentanen Lichtblick.
Keine Nachricht von David! — Abends gemütlich bei Scholz. Sonst
im allgemeinen trüber Stimmung.

4.3.15.
Nicht gearbeitet. Bin moralisch matt; sehe aber die enorme Schwierigkeit meiner Lage ein und bisher bin ich mir noch ganz im Unklaren darüber wie sie zu korrigieren ist. —.

5.3.15.
Sprach heute mit Gürth über meine unwürdige Stellung. Noch keine
Entscheidung. Vielleicht gehe ich als Infantrist an die Front. = .

6.3.15.
Meine Lage ist noch immer unentschieden. Meine Stimmung stark
wechselnd. —

7.3.15.
Lage unverändert; unbehaglich. Bin mir noch ganz im Unklaren über eine geeignete Veränderung. Jetzt bricht wieder starken
Frost herein! Sehr zur Unzeit! Fühle mich nicht wohl. Bin sozusagen seelisch abgespannt, sehr abgespannt. Was dagegen zu machen
ist?? Ich werde von widerlichen Umständen aufgezehrt. Das ganze

covery. It's been a long time since I have felt as abandoned by all the good spirits as I do now. Only do not lose yourself!!—.—

28.2.15 / 1.3.15.
Did no work. No news from David! Uncertain and shifting mood.

2.3.15. / 3.3.15.
Did no work. Yesterday evening a momentary ray of light. No news from David!—In the evening pleasant time at Scholz's. Otherwise in largely dark mood.

4.3.15.
Did no work. Am morally blank; but I see the enormous difficulty of my position and so far, it is entirely unclear to me to how to correct it. —.

5.3.15.
Talked to Gürth today about my humiliating position. No decision yet. Maybe I will go to the Front with the infantry. = .

6.3.15.
My situation is still not resolved. My mood very variable.—.

7.3.15.
Situation unchanged; uncomfortable. It is still not at all clear to me what would be a suitable alternative. A heavy frost has fallen now. Very untimely! I do not feel well. My soul is worn out, so to speak, very worn out. What to do about it?? I am consumed by annoying circumstances. The entire external life in all its infamy is bursting

äußere Leben mit seiner ganzen Gemeinheit stürmt auf mich ein. Und ich bin innerlich haßerfüllt und kann den Geist nicht in mich einlassen. Gott ist die Liebe. — Ich bin wie ein ausgebrannter Ofen voll Schlacke und Unrat. —

8.3.15.
Lage unentschieden! Unverändert! Depressionen. — =. — —.

9.3.15.
Lage unentschieden! = . Stimmung wachsam aber schlecht. —

10.3.15.
<u>Sehr</u> sinnlich. Unentschlossen. Ruheloser im Geist. = .

11.3.15.
Nicht gearbeitet. Lage unverändert! Nichts als Unannehmlichkeiten. — —.

12.3.15.
Nicht gearbeitet. Viel gedacht. Lage noch unentschieden. — —.

13.3.15.
Lage im Gleichen. Bin ganz unschlüssig. = . —.

14.3.15.
Lage unverändert! —. Nicht gearbeitet. Depression. Der Druck auf die Brust. —.— —

15.3.15.
Traf einen bekannten Einjährigen & besprach mit ihm meine Angelegenheit & werde morgen weiter darüber sprechen. Jetzt

in upon me. And I am filled with hatred and cannot let the spirit enter me. God is love.—I am like a burnt-out oven, full of slag and dung.—

8.3.15.

Situation unresolved! Unchanged! Depressions.— =. — —.

9.3.15.

Situation unresolved! = . Mood wary but dark. —

10.3.15

<u>Strongly</u> sexually aroused. Undecided. Restless in spirit. = .

11.3.15.

Did no work. Situation unchanged! Nothing but unpleasantries. — —.

12.3.15.

No work. Thought a great deal. Situation still unresolved. ——.

13.3.15.

Situation the same. Am quite undecided. = . —.

14.3.15.

Situation unchanged! —. No work. Depression. The pressure on the chest—. ——.

15.3.15.

Met a well-known *Einjährigen* & discussed my situation with him & we will talk further about it tomorrow. Now at least I've caught

habe ich also meine Noten eingeholt. Und noch immer arbeite ich nicht. Werde ich je wieder arbeiten??!!——— ————.

16.3.15.

———.

18.3.15.

Gestern lieben Brief von David! — Bin in die Fabrik umgezogen. David geantwortet. Sehr sinnlich.

19.3.15.

Sprach heute mit Gürth über meine Zukunft. Ohne erfreuliches Resultat. Sehr sinnlich. —.

21.3.15.

Denke daran zu den Kaiserjägern zu gehen da auch Ficker dort ist. Nicht ganz wohl. Nicht gearbeitet. Anhaltend unwohl. ———.

22.3.15.

Unwohl. Gegen Abend besser.

23.3.15.

Sehr sinnlich.

24.3.15.

—. Nicht gearbeitet! Werde ich je wieder arbeiten??!!! —.

27.3.15.

———.———

up on my notes on logic. And still I don't work. Will I ever work again??!!—— ————.

16.3.15.

——.

18.3.15.

Lovely letter from David yesterday!— Moved to the factory. Replied to David. Feeling very aroused.

19.3.15.

Spoke to Gürth today about my future. No gratifying result. Feeling very aroused.

21.3.15.

Thinking of moving to the *Kaiserjägern** since Ficker is there too. Not quite well. Did no work. Persistently unwell. ——.

22.3.15.

Unwell. Better toward evening.

23.3.15

Full of desire.

24.3.15.

—. Did no work! Will I ever work again??!!! —.

27.3.15.

——.——

---

* Rifle regiments. In the Austro-Hungarian army, officially designed by the Imperial and Royal (k.u.k.) military administration as normal infantry regiments.

29.3.15.
Überdrüssig! Von Gemeinheit umgeben. Wie bin ich müde!
———.———.

31.3.15.
Wechselnder Stimmung.

4.4.15. / 5.4.15.
Wechselnder Stimmung.

15.4.15.
Es fällt mir nichts Neues mehr ein! (Gürth von hier abkommandiert.) Ich kann auf nichts mehr Neues denken. Und darauf darf es wohl auch gar nicht ankommen.

16.4.15.
Sehr sinnlich. Onaniere jeden Tag. Lange schon keine Nachricht von David. Ich arbeite. —— ——

17.4.15.
Arbeite.

18.4.15.
Sehr verkühlt!

22.4.15.
Soll jetzt die Oberaufsicht über die ganze Werkstätte kriegen. Neuerliche Unannehmlichkeiten.

24.4.15.
Ich arbeite. —.

29.3.15.

Weary! Surrounded by infamy. How tired I am! ——. ——.

31.3.15.

Variable mood.

4.4.15. / 5.4.15

Variable mood.

15.4.15.

Nothing new occurs to me anymore! (Gürth has been transferred from here.) I can't think of anything new. And that, in any case, is not the issue.

16.4.15.

Strong sexual desire. Masturbate every day. No news from David for a long time. I'm working. — —

17.4.15.

Working.

18.4.15.

Bad cold!

22.4.15.

I have now been assigned to become the supervisor of the whole workshop. New unpleasantries.

24.4.15.

I am working. —.

26.4.15
Arbeite. Sonst meine Tätigkeit sehr unzufriedenstellend.

27.4.15.
Arbeite! In der Fabrik muß ich jetzt meine Zeit verplempern!!! ——

28.4.15.
Arbeite wieder! ——.

29.4.15.
Arbeite. Sonst geht's mir schlecht. Laß dich nur nicht von den gemeinen Menschen bearbeiten.

30.4.15.
Lieben Brief von David!

1.5.15.
Die Gnade der Arbeit! ——

1.5.15.
Alle Theorien die besagen: "Es muß sich doch so verhalten, sonst könnten wir ja nicht philosophieren" oder "sonst könnten wir doch nicht leben" etc. etc. müssen natürlich verschwinden.

5.5.15. / 7.5.15.
Noch immer nicht ernannt! Immer wieder wegen meiner unklaren Stellung. Unannehmlichkeiten. Wenn das noch lange so geht werde ich von hier wegzukommen trachten.

26.4.15.

Working! Otherwise my activity is very unsatisfying.

27.4.15.

Working! Now frittering away my time in the factory!!! ——

28.4.15.

Working again! —.

29.4.15.

Working. Otherwise things are going badly. Do not let yourself be badgered by the mean-spirited rabble.

30.4.15.

Lovely letter from David!

1.5.15.

The blessing of work!—

1.5.15.

All theories that say "This is how it must be, otherwise we could not philosophize" or "otherwise we surely could not live," etc. etc., must of course disappear.

5.5.15. / 7.5.15.

My appointment still hasn't come through! Once again because of my uncertain situation. Unpleasantries. If this goes on much longer I will make an effort to get away from here.

8.5.15. / 10.5.15.
<u>Viel</u> Aufregung! War nahe am <u>Weinen</u>!!!! Fühle mich wie gebrochen & krank! Von Gemeinheit umgeben.

11.5.15.
Nicht gearbeitet.

22.5.15.
Lieben Brief von Russell!

23.5.15.
<u>Die Grenzen meiner Sprache</u> bedeuten die Grenzen meiner Welt.

24.5.15.
Lernte heute den alten Logiker Dziewicki kennen von dem mir Russell in seinem Brief schrieb. Ein netter alter Mann.

25.5.15. / 8.6.15.
Erneuerte Schwierigkeit wegen meiner Beförderung. Werde wahrschenlich von hier wegkommen. Vielfach sehr niedergedrückt. Durch die Gemeinheit meiner Umgebung die mich auf's Schändlichste ausnützt.——.

1.6.15.
Das große Problem, um welches sich alles dreht, was ich schreibe, ist: Ist, a priori eine Ordnung in der Welt, und wenn ja, worin besteht sie?

8.5.15. / 10.5.15.

<u>Much</u> anxiety! I was close to <u>tears</u>!!!! I feel broken & sick! Surrounded by brutality.

11.5.15.

Did no work.

22.5.15.

Lovely letter from Russell!

23.5.15.

The limits of my language mean the limits of my world.

24.5.15.

Made the acquaintance today of the old logician Dziewicki,* whom Russell mentioned in his letter. A nice old man.

25.5.15. / 8.6.15.

Renewed difficulties about my promotion. Will probably take my leave from here. Often *very* depressed. Because of the nastiness of my associates, who take such cruel advantage of me. —.

1.6.15.

The great problem around which everything I write revolves is: Is there a priori an order in the world, and if so, of what does it consist?

---

* M. H. Dziewicki, logician in Kraków, who was an acquaintance of Bertrand Russell's. After the war he wrote Russell that he was happy to meet the young Wittgenstein, who had been in a despondent mood at the time of their meeting and was certain that he would be killed by the Russians (see Baum, *Wittgenstein im Ersten Weltkrieg*, 71).

Du siehst in die Nebelwolke und kannst dir daher einreden, das Ziel sei schon nahe. Aber der Nebel zerrinnt, und das Ziel ist noch nicht in Sicht!

3.6.15.

... *(Daß erlösende Wort ist übrigens hier noch nicht gesprochen.)*

22.6.15.

Arbeite <u>sehr</u> viel! Trotz <u>der widerlichsten</u> Umstände.

You are looking into a fog bank and hence persuade yourself that the goal is near. But the fog lifts, and the goal is not yet in sight.

3.6.15.

... *(The redeeming word, incidentally, has not yet been articulated.)*

22.6.15.

Working very hard! Despite the <u>most</u> repugnant circumstances!

NOTEBOOK 3

March 28 (?), 1916–January 1, 1917

.

EDITOR'S NOTE

T HE NOTEBOOK(S) for July 1915 through early March of 1916 are unfortunately among those that were lost, but the principal events of the nine-month period in question may be deduced from letters and other documents.

In the late autumn, Wittgenstein had been transferred to an artillery workshop train that was based in the small town of Sokal, near Lemberg, where he performed similar duties to those that had been assigned to him in Kraków. During the lull in fighting at this time, Wittgenstein read and wrote a great deal. As for his state of mind, Wittgenstein's biographers point us to a long letter by Dr. Max Bieler, who was in charge of a Red Cross hospital train nearby and made friends with Wittgenstein. The two evidently had daily conversations about philosophical and cultural subjects; for example, Dostoevsky's *Brothers Karamazov*, which they had both read and now discussed avidly. Wittgenstein identified in many ways with the "pure" brother Alyosha, but he also expressed great sympathy for the oldest "sensual" brother Dmitri, who could never disguise his passions. And the work on logic was evidently continuing

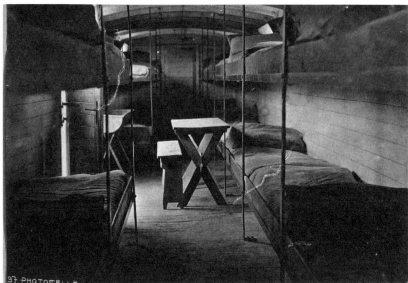

Kowel: Artillery Workshop-Train. Overview of the train, 1916
(Kriegsammlung-Fotos 1914–1918 © Austrian National Library, Vienna)
Kowel: Artillery Workshop-Train, sleeping quarters
(Kriegssammlung-Fotos 1914–1918. © Austrian National Library, Vienna)

with greater speed and confidence: In a letter to Bertrand Russell of October 22, 1915, Wittgenstein announces that he has been working not only very hard but, he feels, with "success":

> I am now at the point of putting the whole thing together in the form of a treatise. Under no circumstances will I publish anything until you have seen it. That cannot, naturally, be till after the war. But who knows whether I shall survive it? In case I don't survive, have my family send you all my manuscripts: among them you will find the most recent summary, written in pencil on loose sheets. It may perhaps cause you some trouble to understand it all, but don't let that put you off.

And he wrote in a similar vein to Frege. Both Russell and Frege wrote back encouraging notes. Russell urged his friend to send on the manuscript to England via a mutual friend in the United States, but given the prolongation of the war and then Wittgenstein's year (1918–1919) as prisoner-of-war in Cassino, Italy, his two mentors were not to see the promised treatise for years. Ray Monk has a telling comment on the irony of the situation:

> If Wittgenstein had followed Russell's suggestion, the work that would have been published in 1916 would have been in many ways, similar to the work we now know as the *Tractatus*. . . . it would have contained almost everything the *Tractatus* now contains—except the remarks at the end of the book on ethics, aesthetics, the soul, and the meaning of life. In a way, therefore, it would have been a completely different work.[1]

True, and what made the decisive difference was surely the experience in battle Wittgenstein was now to undergo.

The relative quiet on the Eastern Front that marked the winter of 1916 came to an abrupt end in late spring, when the Russians were preparing to launch what has come to be known as the Brusilov Offensive against the Austrian armies—one of the most lethal battles of World War I, fought in Southern Galicia in what is now the Ukraine. It was at this time that Wittgenstein finally got his wish to be sent to the front and to face death directly. This was perhaps the major challenge of his life.

Once at the front line, Wittgenstein requested to be assigned to the observation post. This delicately constructed open artillery tower, used for sighting the enemy, was as tall as a tree and inev-

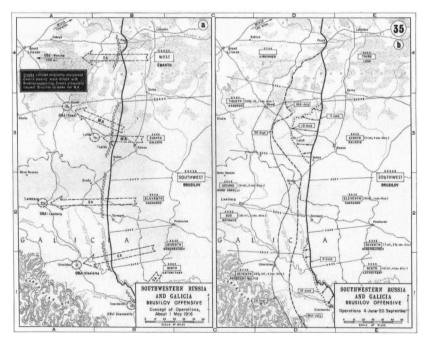

Department of Military Art and Engineering at the U.S. Military Academy, September 1916,
Eastern Front before and after Brusilov Offensive in western Galicia. (West Point)

Artillery observation post
in the Hochwald, 1917
*(First World War, Europeana
Collections 1914–1918. ©
Austrian National Library,
Vienna)*

itably exposed those on top to enemy gunfire. Wittgenstein chose
this post partly to get away from the "cruel, heartless" members
of his unit, men in whom he found it "almost impossible to find a
trace of humanity," and partly to test his courage in the face of fire:
"Perhaps the proximity to death will bring me the light of life! May
God enlighten me!" And indeed Wittgenstein relished his isolated
new post, with its constant threat of being shelled:

> On the observation post, I'm like the prince of the
> enchanted castle. Now all is quiet during the day, but at
> night there must be terrible things going on. Will I be able
> to stand it???? Tonight will tell. God be with me!!

"God be with me!!" Prayer, serious and intimate prayer, not just
to the "Spirit" of Tolstoy's *Gospel* but to God, now becomes central.

And while such prayers are set down on the *verso* of Wittgenstein's notebook—the private side—an interesting change takes place on the *recto* pages. On April 27, 1916, Wittgenstein is still concerning himself with hierarchies and types of simple propositions:

> *Say I wanted to represent a function of three non-interchangeable arguments.*
>
> *ø(x): ø( ), x*
>
> *But should there be any mention of non-interchangeable arguments in logic? If so, this surely presupposes something about the character of reality.*

But nine days later, the day after devising the "enchanted castle" metaphor cited above, we read on the recto:

> *In essence, the whole modern conception of the world is based on the illusion that the so-called* laws *of nature are the explanations of natural phenomena.* [*Tractatus* 6.371]

Wittgenstein was never to waiver from the conviction that there are no "laws of nature" that can explain specific natural phenomena. "Only death," he insists again and again, "gives life its meaning."

Meanwhile, Wittgenstein's platoon was under heavy fire. He had been promoted to *Vormeister* (roughly lance bombardier) and was commended for his behavior on the observation post, which evidently had "a very calming effect" on his comrades. The decoration recommended was the Silver Medal for Valor 2nd Class, a considerable distinction for one of such humble military rank. That decoration was in fact conferred on him in October 1916.

That summer—the summer of 1916, when Wittgenstein came

under direct fire and survived—was his turning point. *"What do I know,"* he writes on July 4, *"about God and the purpose of life?"* and he answers with the now famous litany that begins,

> *I know that this world exists.*
> *That I am placed in it like my eye in its visual field.*
> *That something about it is problematic, which we call its meaning.*
> *That this meaning does not lie in it but outside it.*

This new resignation culminates, the next day, in the response, partly to Schopenhauer, that *"The world is independent of my will. / Even if everything that we wish for were to happen, this would only be, so to speak, a gift of fate, for there is no logical connection between the will and the world that would guarantee it."*

It is an astonishing moment. The Wittgenstein who had long acted on the unstated premise that somehow his will *could* govern his actions, that reason framed the propositions of logic, now writes on July 6, *"to fulfill the purpose of being is to have no other purpose in life than to live."* And on July 8, *"Only he who lives, not in time but in the present, is happy."*

Such privileged moments cannot, of course, last. By July 9, Wittgenstein is once again complaining, "The men are miserable scoundrels," and, a bit later, he admits that, however petty the feeling, he is offended that he has not been invited to use the officers' quarters. But now the painful Austrian retreat through the Carpathian Mountains gets under way. Wittgenstein later recalled that on this long retreat, "he sat utterly exhausted on a horse in an endless column, with the one thought of keeping his seat, since if he fell off, he would be trampled to death." But although he continued to be terrified of being fired at, he writes, "I now have such a strong wish to live! And it is hard to renounce life once one is fond of it."

Outwardly, nothing has really changed: "After a three-day-long train journey, we are crossing the marsh into the firing line. Not in the best of health and sick to my soul as a result of the bigotry and meanness of my compatriots." And a few days later, "I am living in sin, hence unhappy."

The change that has occurred is an inward one. It is the recognition that *"ethics cannot be expressed"*: it can only be *shown*, and that the human, psychological "I" is, after all, not at the center of the universe but only a part of it "along with the animals, plants, stones, etc." (2.9.16). Despite all the petty personal headaches, a strange new tolerance begins to manifest itself. In the final entry of Notebook 3—a right-page entry made a few months after the private pages have been left blank, Wittgenstein wonders whether perhaps even the "elementary sin" of suicide is "in itself neither good nor evil?"

...unterscheiden sind nicht mit
...l sonst könnte sie nicht
werden

...Gleichscheinbarkeiten und
soviel zu unterscheiden
als am Sachverhalt zu
den ist. Darum besteht die
Tat.

...nicht mehr + nicht
...zu erkennen als "~ ...

...ist Sachverhalt mit
...einstimmen und nicht
...übereinstimmen.

...könnte auch so heißen:
...wir zwei ...
...mit einem Anderen

GERMAN TEXT *of* NOTEBOOK 3

DRITTES HEFT, MS. 103

28 (?).3.1916–10.1.1917

---

28 (?).3.16.

. . . und müsse mir das Leben nehmen. Ich litt <u>Höllenqualen</u>! Und doch war mir das Bild des Lebens so verlockend daß ich wieder leben wollte. Erst dann werde ich mich vergiften wenn ich mich wirklich vergiften will.

29.3.16.

Viel <u>Ungewohntes</u> zu tun <u>gezwungen</u>. Ich brauche große Kraft das auszuhalten. Oft bin ich der Verzweiflung nahe. Ich habe schon seit mehr als einer Woche nichts mehr gearbeitet. <u>Ich</u> habe <u>keine Zeit</u>! Gott! Aber es ist ja natürlich, denn wenn ich tot sein werde, werde ich auch keine Zeit zum Arbeiten haben. Jetzt Inspektion. Meine Seele schrumpft zusammen. Gott erleuchte mich! Gott erleuchte mich! Gott erleuchte meine Seele.

30.3.16.

Tu Du dein Bestes! Mehr kannst du nicht tun: und sei heiter. Laß' dir an dir selbst genügen. Denn andere werden dich nicht stützen oder doch nur für kurze Zeit! (Dann wirst du diesen lästig werden).

ENGLISH TEXT *of* NOTEBOOK 3

THIRD NOTEBOOK, MS. 103

28 (?).3.1916—10.1.1917

---

28 (?).3.16.

. . . and must take my life. I suffered the <u>tortures of hell</u>! And yet the picture of life was so enticing to me that I wanted once more to live. I will take poison only when I really want to poison myself.

29.3.16.

<u>Forced</u> to do much that is <u>unfamiliar</u>. I need great strength to endure it. Often I am close to despair. I have done no work for more than a week. <u>I</u> have no <u>time</u>! God! But it is, of course, only natural, for when I am dead, I will also have no time to work. Now the inspection. My soul shrivels up. God enlighten me! God enlighten me! God enlighten my soul.

30.3.16.

You must do your best. You cannot do more: and be of good cheer. Be satisfied with yourself. For others will not give you support or only for a short time! (Then you will become a burden to them.)

Hilf dir selbst und hilf anderen mit deiner ganzen Kraft. Und dabei sei heiter! Aber wieviel Kraft soll man für sich und wieviel für die anderen brauchen? <u>Schwer</u> ist es gut zu leben!! Aber das gute Leben ist schön. "Aber nicht mein sondern dein Wille geschehe."

2.4.16.
War krank. Heute noch sehr schwach. Heute sagte mir mein Kommandant er wolle mich in's Hinterland abschieben lassen. Wenn das geschieht werde ich mich umbringen.

6.4.16.
Das Leben ist eine

7.4.16.
Tortur von der man nur zeitweise heruntergespannt wird um für weitere Qualen empfänglich zu bleiben. Ein furchtbares Sortiment von Qualen. Ein erschöpfender Marsch, eine durchhustete Nacht, eine Gesellschaft von Besoffenen, eine Gesellschaft von gemeinen und dummen Leuten. Tue Gutes und freue dich über deine Tugend. Bin krank und habe ein schlechtes Leben. Gott helfe mir. Ich bin ein armer unglücklicher Mensch. Gott erlöse mich und schenke mir den Frieden! Amen.

10.4.16.
Lebe mit Mühe. Bin noch nicht erleuchtet worden. Sah mich heute im Spiegel, ich bin <u>ganz</u> eingefallen! Ich kann ja auch schon lange nicht mehr arbeiten.

Help yourself and help others with all your might. And at the same time be of good cheer. But how much strength should one use for oneself and how much for others? It is <u>difficult</u> to live the good life! But the good life is beautiful. "But not my will but Thine be done."*

2.4.16.

I was sick. Today still very weak. Today my commander said he would have me sent to the interior, away from the Front. If that happens, I will kill myself.

6.4.16.

Life is a

7.4.16.

form of torture from which there is only temporary reprieve until one can be subjected to further torments. A terrible assortment of torments. An exhausting march, a cough-filled night, a company of drunks, a company of mean and stupid people. Do good and be happy about your virtue. I am sick and lead a bad life. God help me. I am a poor unlucky being. God deliver me and grant me peace! Amen.

10.4.16.

I live with difficulty. Have not yet been enlightened. I looked at myself in the mirror today, my cheeks are <u>quite</u> sunken! Then too, I have not been able to work for a long time.

---

* John 6:38, New Testament.

13.4.16.

Taumle und falle noch immer im Dunkel. Bin noch nicht zum Leben erwacht.

15.4.16.

In 8 Tagen gehen wir in Feuerstellung. Möchte es mir vergönnt sein mein Leben in einer schweren Aufgabe auf's Spiel zu setzen!

16.4.16.

Bin seit dem 22.3. vollkommen asexuell. Die letzten Tage Rasttage.

18.4.16.

Morgen oder übermorgen in die Feuerstellung. Also Mut! Gott wird helfen.

20.4.16.

Gott bessere mich! Dann werde ich auch froher werden. Heute wahrscheinlich schon in Feuerstellung. Gott helfe mir.

23.4.16.

Seit ein paar Tagen in Feuerstellung. Den ganzen Tag über schwere körperliche Arbeit außerstande zu denken. Gott helfe mir; ich habe ungeheuer viel zu leiden. Habe heute angesucht auf den Beobachtungsstand zu kommen. Beim Halbzug haßt mich alles weil mich keiner versteht. Und weil ich kein Heiliger bin! Gott helfe mir!

26.4.16.

Die Offiziere der Batterie können mich scheinbar sehr gut leiden. Dies erspart mir manche Unannehmlichkeit. Gott sei gedankt. Dein Wille geschehe! Geh Du deiner Wege! Dein Wille geschehe!

13.4.16.

Still stumbling and falling in the dark. I have not yet awakened to life.

15.4.16.

We will be at the Front in 8 days. May it be granted to me to put my life in play by receiving a difficult assignment!

16.4.16.

Since 22.3. <u>completely</u> asexual. The last few days a time of passage.

18.4.16.

Tomorrow or the day after tomorrow, at the front line. So take <u>courage</u>! God help me.

20.4.16.

God make me a better person! Then I will also be more cheerful. Today probably already at the front line. God help me.

23.4.16.

I've been at the Front for the last few days. The whole long day <u>hard</u> physical labor, which makes it impossible to think. God help me; I have to suffer enormously. I requested to be assigned to the observation post today. In my platoon everyone hates me because no one understands me. And because I am no saint! God help me!

26.4.16.

The officers of my battery evidently like me very much. That saves me from much aggravation. God be thanked. Thy will be done! Go thy ways! <u>Thy</u> will be done!

27.4.16.

Die Mannschaft mit wenigen Ausnahmen haßt mich als Freiwilligen. So bin ich jetzt fast immer umgeben von Leuten die mich hassen. Und dies ist das Einzige womit ich mich noch nicht abfinden kann. Hier sind aber böse, herzlose Menschen. Es ist mir fast unmöglich eine Spur von Menschlichkeit in ihnen zu finden. Gott helfe mir zu leben. Hatte heute eine Ahnung daß heute nacht Alarm sein werde. Und wirklich ist heute nacht Bereitschaft. Gott sei mit mir! Amen.

28.4.16.

Nachts Ruhe. Schrieb an Russell. Hatte heute einen schlechten Traum. Gott schütze mich.

29.4.16.

Nachmittag bei den Aufklärern. Wurden beschossen. Dachte an Gott. <u>Dein</u> Wille geschehe! Gott sei mit mir.

30.4.16.

Gehe heute während eines Feuerüberfalls wieder zu den Aufklärern: Nur Gott braucht der Mensch.

2.5.16.

Habe mich fortwährend gegen die Gemeinheit der Leute zu wehren.

3.5.16.

Habe es schwer! Gott beschütze mich und stehe mir bei. Amen. Möchte der schwerste Kelch an mir vorüber gehen. Aber Dein Wille geschehe. Die Arbeit schläft in meinem Kopfe.

27.4.16.

The platoon, with a few exceptions, hates me because I am a volunteer. So now I am nearly always surrounded by men who hate me. And this is the one thing to which I can't resign myself yet. Here there are cruel, heartless human beings. It is almost impossible for me to find a trace of humanity in them. God help me to live. I had a premonition that there would be an alarm tonight. And really tonight we are on call. God be with me! Amen.

28.4.16.

At night it was quiet. Wrote to Russell. I had a bad dream last night. God protect me!

29.4.16.

To the observation post in the afternoon. We were shot at. Thought of God. Thy will be done! God be with me.

30.4.16.

During an enemy raid today I'm again going to the observation post. Man needs only God.

2.5.16.

I must constantly struggle against the brutality of my fellow soldiers.

3.5.16.

I'm having a hard time! God protect me and stand by me. Amen. May the worst ordeal pass me by. But Thy will be done. My work is asleep inside my head.

4.5.16.

Komme morgen vielleicht auf mein Ansuchen zu den Aufklärern hinauf. Dann wird für mich erst der Krieg anfangen. Und kann sein—auch das Leben! Vielleicht bringt mir die Nähe des Todes das Licht des Lebens! Möchte Gott mich erleuchten! Ich bin ein Wurm aber durch Gott werde ich zum Menschen. Gott stehe mir bei. Amen.

5.5.16.

Bin wie der Prinz im verwünschten Schloß auf dem Aufklärerstand. Jetzt bei Tag ist alles ruhig aber in der Nacht! Da muß es <u>fürchterlich</u> zugehen! Ob ich es aushalten werde???? Die heutige Nacht wird es zeigen. Gott stehe mir bei!!

6.5.16.

Der ganzen Weltanschaung der Modernen liegt diese Täuschung zu Grunde, daß die Sogenannten Naturgesetze die Erklärungen der Naturerscheinungen seien. [6.371]

So bleiben sie bei den "Naturgesetzen" als by etwas Unantastbarem stehen, wie die Älterern by Gott und dem Schicksal. [See 6.372]

Und sie haben ja beide recht und unrecht. Die Alten sind allerdings insofern klarer, als sie einen klaren Abschluß anerkannten, während es bei dem neuen System scheinen soll, als sei alles begründent. [See 6.372]

7.5.16.

Nacht verlief ruhig. Gott sei Dank. Nur ich bin ein Elender.

8.5.16.

Ruhige Nacht. Gott mit mir!

Die Leute mit denen ich beisammen bin sind nicht so sehr

4.5.16.

In response to my request, I may be sent to the observation post tomorrow morning. Then the war will finally begin for me. And— it may be—my life too! Perhaps the proximity to death will bring me the light of life! May God enlighten me! I am a worm but through God I can become a man. May God stand by me. Amen!

5.5.16.

On the observation post, I'm like the prince in the enchanted castle. Now all is quiet during the day, but at night there must be <u>terrible</u> things going on! Will I be able to stand it???? Tonight will tell. God be with me!!

6.5.16.

In essence, the whole modern conception of the world is based on the illusion that the so-called laws of nature are explanations of natural phenomena. [6.371]

So they stop short at the "laws of nature" treating them as something untouchable, just as their ancestors did with God and Fate. [See 6.372]

And in fact both are right and both are wrong. The Ancients were actually clearer, in that they acknowledged a clear-cut limit, while with the new system, it is supposed to look as if everything can be explained. [See 6.372]

7.5.16.

The night passed quietly. Thank God. I alone am a miserable being.

8.5.16.

Quiet night. God be with me!

The men around me are not so much base as they are <u>appallingly</u>

gemein als <u>ungeheuer</u> beschränkt! Das macht den Verkehr mit ihnen fast unmöglich, weil sie einen ewig mißverstehen. Die Leute sind nicht dumm, aber beschränkt. Sie sind in ihrem Kreise klug genug. Aber es fehlt ihnen der Charakter und damit die Ausdehnung. "Alles versteht das rechtgläubige Herz". Kann jetzt nicht arbeiten.

9.5.16.
Hätte jetzt reichlich Zeit und Ruhe zum Arbeiten. Aber es rührt sich nichts. Mein Stoff ist weit von mir entfernt. Der Tod gibt dem Leben erst seine Bedeutung.

10.5.16.
Durch die Gnade Gottes geht es mir jetzt sehr gut. Arbeiten kann ich leider nicht. Aber Dein Wille geschehe! Amen. In der Gefahr wird er mich nicht verlassen!! —.

11.5.16.
Übermorgen Stellungswechsel. Sehr unangenehm! Aber Dein Wille geschehe.

16.5.16.
In der dritten Stellung. Wie immer viel Mühsal. Aber auch große Gnade. Bin schwach wie immer! Kann nicht arbeiten. Schlafe heute im Infanteriefeuer werde wahrscheinlich zu Grunde gehen. Gott sei mit mir! In Ewigkeit Amen. Ich bin ein schwacher Mensch aber Er hat mich bis nun erhalten. Gott sei gelobt in Ewigkeit, Amen. Ich übergebe meine Seele dem Herrn.

limited. This makes it almost impossible to work with them, because they forever misunderstand me. These people are not stupid, just limited. In their own circle they do well enough. But they lack character and hence depth. "Everything can be understood by the right-thinking heart."* Cannot work now.

9.5.16.

I would now have plenty of time and quiet so that I could work. But nothing is budging. My subject is far away from me. Only death gives life its meaning.

10.5.16.

Through the grace of God I am now doing very well. Unfortunately I can't work. But Thy will be done. Amen. In my danger, He will not desert me!! —.

11.5.16.

Day after tomorrow, change of post. Very unpleasant! But Thy will be done.

16.5.16.

On the third post. As always, much hardship. But also a great blessing. I am as weak as always. I cannot work. I will be sleeping tonight under infantry fire, probably, I will go under. God be with me! For eternity Amen. I am a weak human being but He has sustained me thus far. God be praised in eternity, Amen. I give my soul to the Lord.

---

* The citation comes from one of the sermons of the Elder, Father Zossima, in Book 6, Chapter 2 of Dostoevsky, *The Brothers Karamazov.*

21.5.16.

Gott mache aus mir einen bessern Menschen!

25.5.16.

Werden beschossen. Wie Gott will!

27.5.16.

Briefe von Mining und Mama. Heute oder morgen soll russischer Angriff sein. Nun wie Gott will. Ich bin sehr tief in die Sünde gefallen. Aber Gott wird mir vergeben.

28.5.16.

In den letzten Wochen sehr unruhigen Schlaf. Immer träume ich vom Dienst. Träume die mich immer an die Grenze des Erwachens führen. In den letzten 2 Monaten nur 3 Mal onaniert.

Meine Umgebung ekelt mich gegen meinen Willen an. Nicht wie Menschen sondern wie Fratzen erscheinen sie mir oft. Gemeines Gesindel. Ich hasse sie <u>nicht</u> aber sie ekeln mich an. Heute strenge Bereitschaft. Mein Kommandant ist sehr liebenswürdig mit mir. Denke an das Ziel des Lebens. Das ist noch das Beste was du machen kannst. Ich sollte glücklicher sein. Oh, wenn mein Geist stärker wäre!!! Nur Gott mit mir! Amen.

29.5.16.

Gott mit mir.

21.5.16.

God make me a better person!

25.5.16.

Being shelled. As God wills it!

27.5.16.

Letters from Mining and Mama. Today or tomorrow there is to be a Russian attack. As God wills! I have fallen deeply into sin. But God will forgive me.

28.5.16.

In the past few weeks, very disturbed sleep. I am always dreaming of being on duty. Dreams that always bring me to the edge of awakening. I have only masturbated 3 times in the last two months.

My fellow soldiers disgust me against my will.* They often strike me as not even grown-ups but bratty children. A mean-spirited rabble. I do <u>not</u> hate them but they disgust me. Strict on-call duty today. My commander is very gracious to me. I am thinking about the goal of life. That is still the best thing you can do. I should be happier. Oh, if only my spirit were stronger!!! May God be with me! Amen.

29.5.16.

May God be with me.

---

* The reference is to Schopenhauer's theorem that "The world is independent of my will." See the entry for 5.7.16.

4.7.16.

Was weiß ich über Gott und den Zweck des Lebens?

Ich weiß daß diese Welt ist.

Daß ich in ihr stehe wie mein Auge in seinem Gesichtsfeld.

Daß etwas an ihr problematisch ist was wir ihren Sinn nennen.

Daß dieser Sinn nicht in ihr liegt sondern außer ihr. [Vgl. 6.41]

Daß das Leben die Welt ist. [Vgl. 5.621]

Daß mein Wille die Welt durchdringt.

Daß mein Wille gut oder böse ist.

Daß also Gut und Böse mit dem Sinn der Welt irgendwie zusammenhängt.

Den Sinn des Lebens, d.i. den Sinn der Welt, können wir Gott nennen.

Und das Gleichnis von Gott als einem Vater daran knüpfen.

Das Gebet ist der Gedanke an den Sinn des Lebens.

Ich kann die Geschehnisse der Welt nicht nach meinem Willen lenken sondern bin vollkommen machtlos.

Nur so kann ich mich unabhängig von der Welt machen—und sie also doch in gewissem Sinne beherrschen—indem ich auf einen Einfluß auf die Geschehnisse verzichte.

5.7.16

Die Welt ist unabhängig von meinem Willen. [6.373]

Auch wenn alles was wir wünschen, geschähe, so wäre das doch nur sozusagen eine Gnade des Schicksals, denn es ist kein logischer Zusammenhang zwischen Willen und Welt der dies verbürgte und den angenommenen physikalischen könnten wir doch nicht wieder wollen. [6.374]

4.7.16.*

What do I know about God and the purpose of life?

I know that this world exists.

That I am placed in it like an eye in its visual field.

That something about it is problematic, which we call its meaning.

That this meaning does not lie in it but outside it. [Cf. 6.41]

That life is the world. [Cf. 5.621]

That my will penetrates the world.

That my will is good or evil.

That therefore good and evil are somehow connected with the world.

The meaning of life, i.e., the meaning of the world, we can call God.

And to that meaning we can connect the image of God as a Father.

To pray is to think about the meaning of life.

I cannot bend the happenings in the world to my will; I am completely powerless.

I can only make myself independent of the world—and so in a certain sense master it—by renouncing any influence on events.

5.7.16.

The world is independent of my will. [6.373]

Even if everything that we wish for were to happen, this would only be, so to speak, a gift of fate, for there is no logical connection between the will and the world that would guarantee it, and the assumed physical connection is, in turn, one that we could not will. [6.374]

---

* In *Notebooks 1914–1916*, the date for this entry is given as 11.6.16, but the *Nachlass* has corrected the date.

Wenn das gute oder böse Wollen eine Wirkung auf die Welt hat so kann es sie nur auf die Grenzen der Welt haben, nicht auf die Tatsachen, auf das, was durch die Sprache nicht abgebildet, sondern nur in der Sprache gezeigt werden kann. [Vgl. 6.43]

Kurz, die Welt muß dann dadurch überhaupt eine andere werden. [6.43]

Sie muß sozusagen als Ganzes zunehmen oder abnehmen. Wie durch Dazukommen oder Wegfallen eines Sinnes. [Vgl. 6.43]

Wie auch bei Tod die Welt sich nicht ändert, sondern aufhört zu sein. [6.431]

6.7.16.

Kolossale Strapazen im letzten Monat. Habe viel über alles mögliche nachgedacht kann aber merkwürdigerweise nicht die Verbindung mit meinen mathematischen Gedankengängen herstellen.

6.7.16.

Und insofern hat wohl auch Dostoevsky recht wenn er sagt, daß der welcher glücklich ist, den Zweck des Daseins erfüllt.

Oder man könnte auch so sagen, der erfüllt den Zweck des Daseins der keinen Zweck außer dem Leben mehr braucht. Das heißt nämlich, der befriedigt ist.

Die Lösung des Problems des Lebens merkt man am Verschwindes dieses Problems. [6.521]

Kann man aber so leben daß das Leben aufhört problematisch zu sein? Daß man im Ewigen lebt und nicht in der Zeit?

7.7.16.

Aber die Verbindung wird hergestellt werden!

Was sich nicht sagen läßt, läßt sich nicht sagen!

If to will good or evil has an effect on the world, it can only have one on the boundaries of the world, not on the facts, on what cannot be portrayed by language but can only be shown in language. [Cf. 6.43]

In short, the world must then be an entirely different one. [6.43]

The world must, so to speak, wax or wane as a whole. As if by accession or loss of meaning. [Cf. 6.43]

Just as in death, the world does not change but stops being. [6.431]

6.7.16.

Colossal exertions this last month. Have thought a great deal about all sorts of things, but curiously enough cannot establish their connection to my mathematical train of thought.

6.7.16.

And in this respect Dostoevsky too is surely right when he says that he who is happy is fulfilling the purpose of being.

Or one could also say that the person who fulfills the purpose of being, need have no other purpose than to live. That is to say, to be satisfied.

The solution to the problem of life is to be seen in the disappearance of the problem. [See 6.521]

But can one live so that life ceases to be problematic? So that one is living in eternity and not in time?

7.7.16.

But the connection will have been made!

What cannot be said, cannot be said!

8.7.16.

Leider, leider! Ich habe keine Ruhe zum Arbeiten! Arbeiten.

8.7.16.

An einen Gott glauben heißt die Frage nach dem Sinne des Lebens verstehn.

An einen Gott glauben heißt sehen daß es mit den Tatsachen der Welt noch nicht abgetan ist.

An Gott glauben heißt sehen daß das Leben einen Sinn hat.

Die Welt ist mir gegeben, d.h. mein Wille tritt an die Welt ganz von außen als an etwas Fertiges heran.

(Was mein Wille ist, das weiß ich noch nicht.)

Daher haben wir das Gefühl, daß wir von einem fremden Willen abhängig sind.

Wie dem auch sei, jedenfalls sind wir in einem gewissen Sinne abhängig, und das wovon wir abhängig sind können wir Gott nennen.

Gott wäre in diesem Sinne einfach das Schicksal oder, was dasselbe ist: die—von unserem Willen unabhängige—Welt.

Vom Schicksal kann ich mich unabhängig machen.

Es gibt zwei Gottheiten: die Welt und mein unabhängiges Ich.

Ich bin entweder glücklich oder unglücklich, das ist alles. Man kann sagen: gut oder böse gibt es nicht.

Wer glücklich ist, der darf keine Furcht haben. Auch nicht vor dem Tode.

Nur wer nicht in der Zeit, sondern in der Gegenwart lebt, ist glücklich.

Für das Leben in der Gegenwart gibt es keinen Tod.

Der Tod ist kein Ereignis des Lebens. Er ist keine Tatsache der Welt. [Vgl. 6.43.11]

Wenn man unter Ewigkeit nicht unendliche Zeitdauer, sondern Unzeitlichkeit versteht, dann kann man sagen, daß der ewig lebt, der in der Gegenwart lebt. . . . [Vgl. 6.43.11]

8.7.16.

Alas! Alas! I don't have the peace to work.

8.7.16.

To believe in a God means to understand the question about the meaning of life.

To believe in a God means to see that the facts of the world are not the end of the matter.

To believe in a God means to see that life has a meaning.

The world is given to me, i.e., my will enters into the world completely from the outside as into something that is already there.

(As for what my will is, I don't know yet.)

Therefore we have the feeling that we are dependent upon an alien will.

However that may be, we are, in a certain sense, dependent, and what we are dependent upon we can call God.

In this sense God would simply be fate, or, what is the same thing: the world—which is independent of our will.

I can make myself independent of fate.

There are two godheads: the world and my independent I.

I am either happy or unhappy, that's all. One can say: good or evil do not exist.

He who is happy must have no fear. Not even of death.

Only he who lives, not in time but in the present, is happy.

For life in the present there is no death.

Death is not an event in life. We do not live through it in the world. [Cf. 6.43.11]

If eternity is understood, not as infinite temporal duration, but as non-temporality, then one can say that he lives eternally who lives in the present. . . . [See 6.43.11]

Die Furcht von dem Tode ist das beste Zeichen eines falschen,
d.h. schlechten Lebens. . . .
  Lebe glücklich!

9.7.16.
Ärgere dich nicht über die Menschen. Die Menschen sind graue
Schufte. Und doch darfst du dich nicht über sie ärgern. Ihre Worte
dürfen nicht in dich dringen. Wenn sie mich nicht anreden ist es
noch leicht die Ruhe zu bewahren. Aber wenn sie dir gegenüber
frech und grob werden dann wallt es in mir auf. Ärgere dich nicht.
Ärgern nützt dich gar nichts.

14.7.16.
Die Gnade der Arbeit.

16.7.16.
Furchtbare Witterung. Im Gebirge, schlecht, ganz unzureichend
geschützt eisige Kälte, Regen und Nebel. Qualvolles Leben. Furchtbar schwierig sich nicht zu verlieren. Denn ich bin ja ein schwacher
Mensch. Aber der Geist hilft mir. Am besten wär's ich wäre schon
krank dann hätte ich wenigstens ein bißchen Ruhe.

19.7.16.
Ärgere mich noch immer. Bin ein schwacher Mensch.

20.7.16.
Arbeite nur fort damit du gut wirst.

24.7.16.
Werden beschossen. Und bei jedem Schuß zuckt meine Seele
zusammen. Ich möchte so gerne noch weiter leben!

Fear in the face of death is the best sign of a false, i.e., a bad, life.
. . .

Live happily!

9.7.16.

Don't let the men in the regiment annoy you. The men are miserable scoundrels. But still you must not let yourself get annoyed with them. Their words must not penetrate your being. When they don't address me, it remains easy to keep the peace. But when they are rude and crude to me, I boil up. Don't get angry. Getting angry does you no good.

14.7.16.

The blessing of work.

16.7.16.

Terrible weather. It's bad in the mountains, not sufficiently sheltered, icy cold, rain, and fog. An agonizing life. It's terribly hard not to lose oneself. For I am, after all, a weak human being. But the spirit helps me. The best thing would be if I were already sick, then at least I would have a little peace.

19.7.16.

I still get angry. I'm a weak human being.

20.7.16.

Just keep working so that you will become good.

24.7.16.

We're being shelled. And at every shot my soul contracts. I would like so much to keep on living!

24.7.16.

Die Welt und das Leben sind Eins. [5.621]

Das physiologische Leben ist natürlich nicht "das Leben." Und auch nicht das psychologische. Das Leben, ist die Welt.

Die Ethik handelt nicht von der Welt. Die Ethik muß eine Bedingung der Welt seien, wie die Logik.

Ethik und Aesthetik sind Eins. [Vgl. 6.421]

26.7.16.

Rührenden Brief von David. Er schreibt, sein Bruder sei in Frankreich gefallen. Schrecklich! Dieser liebe freundliche Brief öffnet mir die Augen darüber wie ich hier in der Verbannung lebe. Es mag eine heilsame Verbannung sein aber ich fühle sie jetzt als Verbannung. Ich bin unter lauter Larven verbannt und muß mit diesen unter den widerlichsten Umständen leben. Und in dieser Umgebung soll ich ein gutes Leben führen und mich läutern. Aber das ist furchtbar schwer! Ich bin zu schwach. Ich bin zu schwach! Gott helfe mir.

29.7.16.

Wurde gestern beschossen. War verzagt! Ich hatte Angst vor dem Tode! Solch einen Wunsch habe ich jetzt zu leben! Und es ist schwer auf das Leben zu verzichten wenn man es einmal gern hat. Das ist eben "Sünde", unvernünftiges Leben, falsche Lebensauffassung. Ich werde von Zeit zu Zeit zum Tier. Dann kann ich an nichts denken als an essen, trinken, schlafen. Furchtbar! Und dann leide ich auch wie ein Tier, ohne die Möglichkeit innerer Rettung. Ich bin dann meinen Gelüsten und meinen Abneigungen preisgegeben. Dann ist an ein wahres Leben nicht zu denken.

24.7.16.

The world and life are one. [5.621]

    The physiological life is naturally not "life." And neither is the psychological life. Life is the World.

    Ethics does not deal with the world. Ethics must be a condition of the world, like logic.

    Ethics and aesthetics are one. [See 6.421]

26.7.16.

Very moving letter from David. He writes that his brother was killed in action in France. Terrible! This sweet, affectionate letter opens my eyes to how I live here in <u>exile</u>. It may be a healthy exile but I feel it now as an exile. I am exiled among a bunch of worms and must live with them under the most disgusting circumstances. And in this environment I am supposed to lead a good life and purify myself. But it is <u>terribly</u> hard! I am too weak. God help me.

29.7.16.

Yesterday, I was fired at. I fell apart! I was afraid of death! I now have such a strong wish to live! And it is hard to renounce life once one is fond of it. That is precisely what "sin" is, an unreasonable life, a wrong view of life. From time to time I become an <u>animal</u>. Then I can think of nothing but eating, drinking, sleeping. Terrible! And then I also suffer like an animal, without the possibility of internal salvation. I am then at the mercy of my appetites and aversions. Then an authentic life cannot even be considered.

30.7.16.

Komisch: Heute ärgere ich mich darüber daß ich bei der Infanterie wo ich jetzt in Verpflegung bin nicht Offiziersmenage bekomme wie mir anfangs in Aussicht gestellt wurde. Ich benehme mich also im höchsten Grade kindisch und schlecht. Aber trotzdem kann ich meinen Ärger über das erlittene Unrecht nicht bemeistern. Immer wieder muß ich daran denken, und wie ihm etwa abgeholfen werden könnte. So dumm ist der Mensch.

30.7.16.

Der erste Gedanke bei der Aufstellung eines allgemeinen ethischen Gesetzes von der Form "Du sollst..." ist: "Und was dann, wenn ich est nicht tue?"

Es ist aber klar, daß die Ethik nichts mit Strafe und Lohn zu tun hat.

[...]

Immer wieder komme ich darauf zurück, daß einfach das glückliche Leben gut, das unglückliche schlecht ist. Und wenn ich mich jetzt frage aber <u>warum</u> soll ich gerade glücklich leben, so erscheint mir das von selbst als eine tautologische Fragestellung; es scheint, daß das glückliche Leben von selbst als eine tautologische Fragestellung; es scheint, daß sich das glückliche Leben von selbst rechtfertigt, daß es das einzig richtige Leben <u>ist</u>.

Alles dies ist eigentlich in gewissem Sinne tief geheimnisvoll! Es ist <u>klar</u>, daß sich die Ethik nicht ausprechen <u>läßt</u>! [Vgl. 6.421] ...

Die Ethik ist transcendent. [Vgl. 6.421]

2.8.16.

... Ja, meine Arbeit hat sich ausgedehnt von den Grundlagen der Logik zum Wesen der Welt.

30.7.16.

Funny: Today I am annoyed that in the infantry, to which I am now assigned, I cannot qualify for the officers' quarters, as had earlier been promised would be the case. I therefore behave as childishly and badly as possible. Even so, I cannot control my irritation about the injustice endured. Again and again, I dwell on it, and wonder what I could do to remedy it. That's how stupid man is.

30.7.16.

The first thought in response to the establishment of a general ethical law in the form "Thou shalt . . ." is "And what, then, if I don't do it?"

But it is clear that ethics has nothing to do with punishment or reward.

[. . .]

Again and again I come back to this! Simply that the happy life is good, the unhappy bad. And if I now ask myself: but why should I live happily, then this seems in itself to be a tautological question; it appears, that the happy life is justified in itself, it seems that it is the only right life.

All this is in some sense very mysterious! It is clear that ethics cannot be expressed! [Cf. 6.421] . . .

Ethics is transcendent. [See 6.421]

2.8.16.

. . . Yes, my work has expanded its reach from the foundations of logic to the nature of the world.

6.8.16.

Nach 3 Tagen Bahnfahrt auf dem Marsch in die Feuerstellung. Nicht bei bester Gesundheit und durch die Borniertheit und Gemeinheit meiner Umgebung seelisch marod. Gott gib mir Kraft, innere Stärke, der seelischen Krankheit zu trotzen. Gott erhalte mich bei frohem Mute.

7.8.16.

Das Ich ist kein Gegenstand.

11.8.16.

Lebe in der Sünde dahin, d.h. unglücklich. Bin verdrossen, freudlos. Lebe mit meiner ganzen Umgebung in Unfrieden.

11.8.16.

Jedem Gegenstand stehe ich objektiv gegenüber. Dem Ich nicht.

Es gibt also wirklich eine Art und Weise, wie in der Philosophie <u>in einem nicht psychologischen Sinne</u> vom Ich die Rede sein kann und muß. [Vgl. 5.641]

12.8.16.

Du weißt was du zu tun hast um glücklich zu leben; warum tust du es nicht? Weil du unvernünftig bist. Ein schlechtes Leben ist ein unvernünftiges Leben. Es kommt darauf an sich nicht zu ärgern.

12.8.16.

Das Ich tritt in die Philosophie dadurch ein, daß die Welt <u>meine</u> Welt ist. [Vgl. 5.641] . . .

Das hängt damit zusammen, daß kein Teil unserer Erfahrung a priori ist. [Vgl. 5.634]

Alles was wir sehen, könnte auch anders sein.

6.8.16.

After a three-day-long train journey, we are crossing the marsh into the firing line. Not in the best of health and sick to my soul as a result of the bigotry and meanness of my compatriots. God give me power, the inner strength, to defy this soul-sickness. God maintain me in good spirits.

7.8.6.

The I is not an object.

11.8.16.

I am living in sin, hence unhappy. I'm morose, joyless. I'm at strife with my entire company.

11.8.16.

I can objectively confront every object. But not the "I."

So there really is an art and method by which philosophy can and must come to terms with the "I" in a non-psychological sense. [Cf. 5.641]

12.8.16.

You know what you have to do in order to live happily; why don't you do it? Because you are irrational. A bad life is an unreasonable life. Everything depends on not letting yourself get angry.

12.8.16.

The "I" makes its appearance in philosophy by means of the idea that the world is my *world.* [See 5.641] . . .

This is connected with the fact that none of our experience is a priori. [See 5.634]

Everything we see could also be otherwise.

Alles was wir überhaupt beschreiben können, könnte auch anders sein. [Vgl. 5.634]

13.8.16.
Kämpfe noch vergebens gegen meine schwache Natur. Gott stärke mich!

13.8.16.
Angenommen, der Mensch könnte seinen Willen nicht betätigen, müßte aber aller Not dieser Welt leiden, was könnte ihn dann glücklich machen?

Wie kann der Mensch überhaupt glücklich sein, da er doch die Not dieser Welt nicht abwehren kann?

Eben durch das Leben der Erkenntnis.

Das gute Gewissen ist das Glück, welches das Leben der Erkenntnis gewährt.

Das Leben der Erkenntis ist das Leben, welches glücklich ist, der Not der Welt zum Trotz.

Nur das Leben ist glücklich, welches auf die Annehmlichkeiten der Welt verzichten kann.

Ihm sind die Annehmlichkeiten der Welt nur so viele Gnaden des Schicksals.

19.8.16.
Von Gemeinheit umgeben! Soll in absehbarer Zeit zum Kader in's Hinterland abgehen. Bin froh darüber. Von Gemeinheit umgeben. Gott wird helfen.

10.1.1917.
Wenn der Selbstmord erlaubt ist, dann ist alles erlaubt.
Wenn etwas nicht erlaubt ist, dann ist der Selbstmord nicht erlaubt.

Everything we can actually describe could also be otherwise. [See 5.634]

13.8.16.

Still fighting in vain against my weak nature. God strengthen me!

13.8.16.

Suppose that man could not exercise his will, but had to suffer all the misery of his world, then what could make him happy?

How can man be happy anyway since he cannot ward off the misery of this world?

Precisely through the life of understanding.

A good conscience is the happiness that the life of understanding preserves.

The life of understanding is the life that is happy despite the misery of the world.

The only life that is happy is the life that can renounce the conveniences of the world.

To it, the conveniences of the world are only so many gifts of fate.

19.8.16.

Surrounded by viciousness! Sometime soon I am supposed to return to behind the lines to my regiment. I'm glad about it. Surrounded by viciousness. God will help.

10.1.1917.

If suicide is allowed then everything is allowed.

If anything is not allowed then suicide is not allowed.

Dies wirft ein Licht auf das Wesen der Ethik. Denn der Selbstmord ist sozusagen die elementare Sünde.

Und wenn man ihn untersucht, so ist es, wie wenn man den Quecksilberdampf untersucht, um das Wesen der Dämpfe zu erfassen.

Oder ist nicht auch der Selbstmord an sich weder gut noch böse!

This throws a light on the nature of ethics, for suicide is, so to speak, the elementary sin.

And when one investigates it, it is like investigating mercury vapor in order to comprehend the nature of vapors.

Or is even suicide in itself neither good nor evil?

AFTERWORD

A NOTE ON THE MANUSCRIPT

It is strange what a relief it is for me to write in secret
script of certain things that I would not like to be legible.
WITTGENSTEIN, 1929

AT THE TIME of Wittgenstein's death in 1951, only a single work of his had been published: the *Tractatus Logico-Philosophicus* (1922). His second major work, the *Philosophical Investigations*, was almost ready for publication, but Wittgenstein, as was his habit, was still tinkering with it when he died. Reluctant to consider any of his texts sufficiently "finished," he left behind approximately 20,000 pages of manuscript and typescript. In his will, his three literary executors, all of them former students and devoted disciples, were given the following directive:

> I give to Mr. R[ush] Rhees, Miss [Elizabeth] Anscombe and
> Professor G. H. von Wright of Trinity College Cambridge
> all the copyright in all my unpublished writings and also
> the manuscripts and typescripts thereof to dispose of as
> *they think best* but subject to any claim by anybody else to
> the custody of the manuscripts and typescripts.

> I intend and desire Mr. Rhees, Miss Anscombe and
> Professor von Wright shall publish as many of my unpub-
> lished writings as they see fit, but I do not wish them to
> incur expenses in publications which they do not expect to
> recoup out of royalties or other profits.[2]

What a directive! The *Nachlass*, as the collection of Wittgenstein's notebooks, ledgers, typescripts, and collections of clippings
was to be called, was further complicated by the fact that although
Wittgenstein always wrote in German, his Cambridge and other
lectures in England were given—and hence recorded—in English.
The *Philosophical Investigations*, for example, was ready to be published in a bilingual edition—Anscombe had translated the latest
version six years earlier in 1945—but she and Rhees remembered
that Wittgenstein had wanted the book to include his recent work
on psychological concepts, and so they added the relevant pages,
which became Part II. Anscombe, as Christian Erbacher tells us
in his excellent *Wittgenstein's Heirs and Editors*, thought this later
typescript "transcends everything [Wittgenstein] ever wrote," but
later scholars came to question whether it had been Wittgenstein's
intent to include this manuscript in the *Investigations*, and in the
fourth edition (2009),[3] what was known as Part II has been sepa-
rated from the body of the text of the *Investigations* and renamed
"Philosophy of Psychology: A Fragment."

From 1951 on, in any case, the three editors began to assemble the various manuscripts and see to their publication. They did
not always agree on the sequence or on the importance of this or
that manuscript, and, as Erbacher tells it, "Until the mid-1960s,
the literary executors' handling of the material documents of Wittgenstein's writings might have driven professional historians and
librarians to despair":

Rhees and Anscombe kept the manuscripts and typescripts at their homes, working with them, sometimes
writing notes in them and exposing them to the dangers
of daily life—sometimes with disastrous consequences:
the typescripts from which PI 1953 was typeset were lost;
Anscombe is said to have burnt a section that referred to a
then-living person; Rhees's dog tried to eat one of the manuscripts; and Rhees himself lost the original of the [G. E.]
Moore volume in a telephone booth at Paddington Station
in London.[4]

It is in this context that the trajectory of Wittgenstein's *Private
Notebooks* must be understood. Shortly after Wittgenstein's death,
his sister Margarete Stonborough invited the three literary executors to Austria to show them the manuscripts she possessed and to
discuss publication. Among the papers were three notebooks written between 1914 and the end of 1916, when Wittgenstein was serv-
ing in the Austro-Hungarian infantry on the Eastern Front:

> *MS 101. 9 August 1914–30 October 1914*
> *MS 102. 30 October 1914–22 June 1915*
> *MS 103. 28 (?) March 1916–10 January 1917*

Note the nine-month gap between the second and third notebooks, which indicates a lost notebook. There were, moreover, evidently three or four other notebooks from the war period that were
either lost or destroyed.[5]

In 1954, having edited Wittgenstein's *Remarks on the Foundations of Mathematics*, the executors decided to publish the 1914–1916
notebooks next, because they shed so much light on the embryonic
Tractatus. But they chose only those sections they regarded as phil-

osophically relevant, and, not wishing to violate the privacy of their mentor, they excluded the entire body of coded entries that filled each left-hand page (the verso) of the notebooks. Code, in other words, meant "Keep out." Accordingly, the volume called *Notebooks 1914–1916*, first published by Blackwell in 1961 and available now from the University of Chicago Press in its 1979 second edition, reproduces the right-hand (recto) pages of the notebooks only. Indeed, there is no indication in *Notebooks 1914–1916* that there is anything missing.

For decades, the decision to leave the coded personal notebooks unpublished held. Anscombe was adamant on the subject. When, in 1958, Wittgenstein's friend Paul Engelmann consulted her on the possibility of publishing his letters from Wittgenstein and reminiscences of their time together in his native Olmütz in 1915–1916, Anscombe responded:

> If by pressing a button it could have been secured that people would not concern themselves with his personal life, I should have pressed the button. . . . Further, I must confess that I feel deeply suspicious of anyone's claim to have understood Wittgenstein. That is perhaps because . . . I am very sure that I did not understand him.[6]

Rush Rhees agreed. In the 1960s, when the executors were trying to decide how to handle the coded remarks for the new Cornell microfilm edition of the *Nachlass*, Rhees remarked:

> I wished (and do) that W. had not written those passages. I do not know why he wanted to; but I think I do understand in a way, and I understand then also why he chose this ambiguous medium. I fear especially that if they are

published, they will be published by themselves—not in
the contexts (repeat: contexts) in which they were written; so that what was a minor and occasional undertone
to Wittgenstein's life and thinking, will appear as a dom-
inant obsession.[7]

The "minor and occasional undertone" to which Rhees here alludes
no doubt refers to Wittgenstein's expression of sexual (specifically,
homosexual) desire—here always oblique but unmistakable, as
when, in an entry of December 21, 1914, he writes of kissing the
letter he has just received from his adored Cambridge friend David
Pinsent. The Notebooks dutifully note every time their author mas-
turbates, and there are telling allusions to gay rendezvous, as when
Wittgenstein records his frequent visits to the baths in Kraków or
refers to his repeated and unspecified "sins."

Such personal material, Rhees and Anscombe felt, was not
appropriate for publication: In the 1960s, a taboo on homosexual
acts was still largely operative. The solution, for the Cornell project,
was thus to microfilm the *Nachlass* in a two-step procedure: First, a
microfilm of the entire manuscript was produced, and then a copy
was made in which the coded remarks were blacked out. Scholars
who visited the Cornell archive were allowed access to this expur-
gated copy only.

The third executor, von Wright, who had returned to his native
Finland, took a somewhat different position. More familiar with
the history and culture of the Austro-Hungarian Empire than
either the American Rhees or the English Anscombe, he came to
understand that Wittgenstein was intimately bound to the Vienna
of his birth—a Vienna that was, in the early twentieth century,
one of the great centers for avant-garde literature, music, and
art, as well as the social sciences. The seemingly casual aphoris-

tic remarks, scattered throughout Wittgenstein's manuscripts, von Wright discovered, were often central to his thinking. By the early 1970s, von Wright had assembled some 1,500 general remarks from different manuscripts, which were to find their way into the volume called *Vermischte Bemerkungen* (1977)—*Culture and Value* in English. This bilingual volume, translated by Peter Winch, has gone through many editions, the most recent in 1998, and is at this writing one of Wittgenstein's most popular books even though it is, strictly speaking, not a book "by" Wittgenstein at all.

In this context, it was inevitable that Wittgenstein's coded remarks, scattered throughout the *Nachlass*, but especially the entries in the private World War I notebooks, would generate a great deal of interest. In the 1980s, Wilhelm Baum, who had transcribed these notebooks from the manuscripts held at the then newly founded Tübingen Archive, brought out, first, a journal article in the *Zeitschrift für Katholische Theologie* (1985), and then a book reproducing the entire corpus of coded remarks in MSS. 101–103, under the title *Geheime Tagebücher*, published in Vienna in 1991. Almost immediately, Italian and Spanish editions followed, and a French one called *Carnets secrets* was undertaken by the Wittgensteinian philosopher Jean-Pierre Cometti.[8]

Anscombe was evidently appalled and filed a lawsuit to the effect that the German edition was unauthorized and should be banned. Baum later got around this ban by changing his title to *Wittgenstein im Ersten Weltkrieg* (2014) and providing documentation to justify his publication. But the stigma from Cambridge was so great that Baum's book, under either title, received little attention, and it is currently out of print. By the early 1990s, however, both Brian McGuinness and Ray Monk had published their seminal biographies: It was Monk's *Ludwig Wittgenstein: The Duty of Genius* that brought me to Wittgenstein in the first place. Both biographers refer to and quote extensively from the war notebooks; indeed, McGuinness's long Chapter 7, "The War 1914–1918," is based heavily on the day-by-day account in the diary.

At the time, I assumed there would soon be an English translation, as was the case with *Culture and Value* or the box file of typed fragments published in 1967 as *Zettel*. But no such thing happened. At this writing in 2021, there is no English translation of the *Private Notebooks* or, for that matter, an authorized German text. One can, of course, read the originals in the Bergen [Norway] Nachlass Edition (BNE) of the *Nachlass*, transcribed by an outstanding team of editors under the direction of Alois Pichler; indeed, the *Nachlass* is one of the great scholarly digital projects of our time. But readers who read no German have no access to these texts or, for that matter, to the important—and again partially coded—*Cambridge Notebooks, 1930–1932/1936–1937*, edited by Ilse Somavilla for the Institute of Research at the Brenner Archive in Innsbruck in 1999. The 1930s notebooks are available in a French edition called *Carnets de Cambridge et de Skjolden*, again translated by Jean-Pierre Cometti, but although new volumes of the later writings—say, on psychology or mathematics—continue to be published, the World War I private notebooks are still unavailable.[9]

The question, of course, is why. One can only speculate, but I think the answer has to do with both Wittgenstein's nationality and his sexuality, especially as that sexuality was understood (or misunderstood) in the Cambridge of his day. And here we must remember that if the *Tractatus* belongs to the Vienna period of Wittgenstein's life, all the post-1929 writings, even though written in German, were first published in the United Kingdom, and the many Cambridge lectures, seminal as they are to the conception of the *Philosophical Investigations*, were of course delivered in

English and transcribed by Wittgenstein's colleagues and students in English.

In the Anglophone world, Wittgenstein tends to be regarded as an English philosopher, to be read against Bertrand Russell, G. E. Moore, A. N. Whitehead, Frank Ramsey, and others. The early influence of Spinoza, Schopenhauer, and Frege (and later of Kant) is certainly acknowledged, but the British milieu is taken as central. Even the *Tractatus,* after all, was first known in the C. K. Ogden translation for Routledge (London), published at the behest of, and with an introduction by, Bertrand Russell, after a number of Viennese publishers had turned down the manuscript. Russell's Introduction was not uncritical: "The whole subject of ethics," he complained, "is placed by Mr. Wittgenstein in the mystical, inexpressible region. Nevertheless he is capable of conveying his ethical opinions."[10] This rather sardonic comment infuriated Wittgenstein, but he understood how much he owed his first mentor. And further: He owed the awarding of the PhD for the *Tractatus* to that other Cambridge philosopher, G. E. Moore.

Indeed, all the subsequent men in Wittgenstein's life, from Francis Skinner to Ben Richards, were English-speaking, as were his good friends and disciples such as Norman Malcolm and J. O. C. Drury. In the United States, moreover, Wittgenstein's philosophy—primarily the later work—has been channeled by the very forceful presence of Stanley Cavell at Harvard. A number of recent books on Wittgenstein openly take their cue from Cavell's representation of Wittgenstein's ordinary-language philosophy and ethics.[11]

In the Oxbridge of the post–World War II years—and, for that matter, in the leading American universities—the study of philosophy has been regarded as an abstract and conceptual discipline, rigorous in its reasoning and quite unrelated to issues of individual biography. Ironically, toward the end of the century, when the two excellent English biographies of Wittgenstein (McGuinness, 1988; Monk, 1990) were published, dozens of memoirs, fictions, and even films about the elusive philosopher began to flood the market. But from the perspective of serious philosophy, the productions of a Terry Eagleton (the novel *Saints and Scholars*, 1987) or a Derek Jarman (the film *Wittgenstein*, 1993) were considered ancillary, if not frivolous.

From January 1929 on, in any case, when John Maynard Keynes wrote to his wife, Lydia Lopokova, "Well, God has arrived. I met him on the 5.15 train," Wittgenstein belonged to Cambridge. (Emblematically, the manuscript of the *Private Notebooks* belongs to the Wren Library at Trinity College.) And at Cambridge, the original reticence of his executors as to his private life refused to fade. Neither the *Oxford Handbook of Wittgenstein* (2011) nor the more recent *Cambridge Companion to Wittgenstein* (2018) devote more than a few pages to their subject's personal life. In his extraordinarily detailed biography, Brian McGuinness avoids all questions of sexuality, and even Ray Monk remarks, with respect to the diaries:

> What the coded remarks reveal is that Wittgenstein was uneasy, not about homosexuality, but about sexuality itself. Love, whether of a man or a woman, was something he treasured. He regarded it as a gift, almost a divine gift. But . . . he sharply differentiated love from sex. Sexual arousal, both homo- and heterosexual, troubled him enormously. He seemed to regard it as incompatible with the sort of person he wanted to be.

> What the coded remarks also reveal is the extraordi-

nary extent to which Wittgenstein's love life and his sexual life went on only in his imagination.[12]

The difficulty with this account is that, as Monk's own biography
makes clear, women played almost no role in Wittgenstein's life.
His one brief heterosexual "affair"—with a Swiss woman, Margue-
rite Respinger, whom he had met through his sister Gretl in Vienna
in the late 1920s—came to a decisive end when he explained to her
that, if they were to wed, "he had a Platonic, childless marriage in
mind."[13]

I know of no other woman Wittgenstein can be said to have
loved; indeed, he traveled almost exclusively in male circles. Nor do
I think that in the case of the men he loved, from David Pinsent
to Ben Richards, and especially Francis Skinner (with whom he
acknowledged having a physical relationship), Wittgenstein sepa-
rated sex from love and loved only in his imagination. Somehow,
even Monk, who seems to understand Wittgenstein so perfectly,
cannot reconcile himself to his subject's queerness. Meanwhile in
Vienna, publication and translation were held up for different reasons. In the late 1920s, before Wittgenstein's return to Cambridge,
the *Tractatus* served as a kind of Bible to the Vienna Circle of logical empiricists, founded in the late 1920s by Moritz Schlick. Wittgenstein attended some of their meetings but was always suspicious
of what he felt was their overcommitment to system. During the
Nazi period leading up to World War II, and especially after the
murder of Schlick by a deranged student in 1936, the Vienna Circle
dispersed, many of its members taking up residence in the United
States, and it was not until the 1990s that the so-called Vienna Edition of Wittgenstein's *Collected Works*, first undertaken by Michael
Nedo, began to appear: that edition is still not complete.

Allan Janik and Stephen Toulmin's *Wittgenstein's Vienna*[14] has been seminal in reminding readers that Wittgenstein was, after all, a product of a very particular Central European culture—and that this culture was not English. And in the past two decades, at the Brenner Archive at Innsbruck, Wittgenstein's work has been actively published and studied. In 2019, for example, Ilse Somavilla and Carl Humphries published an important collection of essays (some in English) on the *Notebooks 1930–1932/1936–1937* called *Wittgensteins Denkbewegungen* [*Modes of Thinking*].[15] Indeed, seventy years after his death, in a process that reminds me of Samuel Beckett's vexed relationship to his native Ireland, Wittgenstein is finally being reclaimed by the country of his birth.*

But the Austrian circle has had similar difficulties as the English with Wittgenstein's sexuality: It is as if his admirers consider him to be some sort of saint—a pure being—and hence above and beyond "normal" sexual needs, much less same-sex relationships. And further they argue that, whatever his sexuality may have been, it can have no relevance to the discussion of logic and representation, to "forms of life," or to the ethical considerations in the *Tractatus* and the *Notebooks 1914–1916*, which was its first sketch.

Wittgenstein himself contributed to this state of affairs. Like his contemporary Marcel Proust, who made his narrator both anti-Semitic and homophobic even though he himself was Jewish and homosexual, Wittgenstein wanted to distance himself from issues of sexuality as well as of questions of national identity. It was part

---

* The Austrian Ludwig Wittgenstein Society, founded in 1974, holds annual international meetings and a summer school in Kirchberg-am-Wechsel, where Wittgenstein taught elementary school in the early 1920s. Meanwhile, in Vienna, recent studies of the *Wiener Kreis* have sparked renewed interest in Wittgenstein, and there is now a very active and independent *Wittgenstein Initiative*, founded by Radmila Schweitzer, which holds lectures, symposia, and exhibitions, and publishes new scholarship on philosophical, cultural, and biographical issues relating to Wittgenstein.

of his youthful training in a Vienna where external form, role playing, and secrecy were so important. He remains to this day an enigmatic figure, challenging us to make sense of his anomalies— anomalies that are especially vivid in the *Private Notebooks of 1914–1916*, here presented for the first time in the 100-plus years since they were written.

ACKNOWLEDGMENTS

THIS BOOK owes its existence to Yunte Huang, professor of comparative literature at UC–Santa Barbara, noted author, and dear friend, who happened to be visiting me one day in mid-August 2020 and heard me say how incredulous I was to discover that there was no English translation of Wittgenstein's private notebooks, written in code during World War I, which I had been reading in a German edition, long out of print, called *Geheime Tagebücher.* Yunte thought for a moment and said, "I think this is something that Bob [Robert Weil, editor in chief of Liveright] might be interested in." I knew of Robert Weil as a brilliant, exacting "hands-on" editor in the tradition of Maxwell Perkins (an all but extinct species today), and Yunte pointed out that Weil was fluent in German and had published writers like Joseph Roth, Robert Musil, and Michael Hofmann. But Wittgensteins's private notebooks? Wasn't it too specialized a project?

The very next day I got a note from Bob Weil, expressing "keen interest" in the project and asking me for a sample translation and rationale. I stayed up late doing a short translation and mailed it off. By Labor Day I had a contract for an English edition. I could hardly believe my good fortune. Bob understood that these aphoristic Notebooks had an appeal well beyond the narrow circle of professional philosophers, and he helped me to address that wider audience. His own deep learning, astonishing literary judgment, and close reading of the manuscript have been invaluable. And Bob's very talented editorial aide, Haley Bracken, performed wonders putting the manuscript in final shape. Steve Attardo produced a beautiful and discerning cover design, of which I am proud.

I want to thank the remarkable Wittgenstein scholars, colleagues, and friends who advised me on the project: Kurt Olaf Åmås, Nicolas Bell, Charles Bernstein, Gerald Bruns, Johanna Drucker, Craig Dworkin, Christoph Erbacher, Thomas Harrison, James Klagge, Efrain Kristal, Peter Middleton, Alan Sandry, Alfred Schmid, John Solt, Ilse Somavilla, David Stern, Pierre and Françoise Stonborough, Robert von Hallberg, and Karen Zumhagen-Yekplé. Allan Janik, the author of *Wittgenstein's Vienna,* gave excellent "inside" advice as to how to proceed, and Alois Pilcher, the head of the Wittgenstein Archives at the University of Bergen in Norway, was kind enough to let me base this translation on his revised transcription of MSS 101, 102, and 103 of the *Nachlass,* listed in the bibliography. Professor Friedrich Stadler, who organized a conference on Wittgenstein and the Wiener Kreis in the summer of 2021, gave me the opportunity to try out some of my ideas on an audience of experts.

Anyone who works on Wittgenstein's personal papers owes a profound debt to Ray Monk, the author of the great biography *Ludwig Wittgenstein: The Duty of Genius*—the book that first aroused my interest in Wittgenstein. Monk's many citations from the private notebooks prompted me to order the German edition, edited by Wilhelm Baum in 1991.

Finally: Radmila Schweitzer, the director of the Wittgenstein Initiative in Vienna, is, in many ways, the coauthor of this edition. She put me in touch with all the relevant scholars, copyright holders, and family members, introduced me to the leading parties involved, advised me at each step of the way, read the entire manuscript, and supplied most of the photographs. Over the past decade, I have attended a number of symposia in Vienna, most of them at Radmila's invitation. And her own catalogue *Die Traktatus Odyssee*, published in 2018, is an invaluable source on Wittgenstein's war years.

As always, my daughters, Nancy and Carey, read the manuscript and gave excellent pointers. This year, all three of us have books in press—a happy thought. Somehow, writing has made the pandemic year 2020 much more bearable for all three of us.

Marjorie Perloff
Pacific Palisades, California

NOTES

Introduction

1. See Monk, *Ludwig Wittgenstein*, 579. Wittgenstein died of colon cancer on April 29, 1951.
2. See Wittgenstein, *Lectures and Conversations on Aesthetics*, 11.
3. Wittgenstein, *Blue and Brown Books*, 28.
4. Wittgenstein, *Notebooks 1914–1916*, 49 (23.5.15), and then in the *Tractatus*, 5.6.
5. Wittgenstein, *Wittgenstein's Lectures Cambridge, 1930–32*, 112.
6. Wittgenstein, *Philosopical Investigations*, §250.
7. Witggenstein, *Wittgenstein's Lectures Cambridge*, 112, 116.
8. Wittgenstein, *Philosophical Investigations*, §43.
9. See Wittgenstein, *Culture and Value*, 28. My translation.
10. Wittgenstein, *Wittgenstein's Lectures Cambridge, 1930–32*, 1.
11. Wittgenstein, *Philosophical Investigations*, §309.
12. Wittgenstein, *Philosophical Investigations*, §498.
13. Wittgenstein, *Culture and Value*, 44.
14. Wittgenstein, *Wittgenstein's Lectures Cambridge, 1930–32*, 24–26.
15. See Perloff, "Becoming a 'Different' Person," in *Edge of Irony*, 153–69.
16. See Wittgenstein, *Notebooks 1914–1916*, 73, 84; *Tractatus*, §6.41.
17. Wittgenstein, *Tractatus*, §7, my translation. The Ogden translation "Whereof one cannot speak, thereof one must be silent" is a very stilted rendering of Wittgenstein's colloquial "Worüber man nicht sprechen kann, darüber muss man schweigen."
18. Drury, "Some Notes on Conversations with Wittgenstein," 94.
19. Wittgenstein, *Philosophical Investigations*, §268.
20. Wittgenstein, *Zettel*, §717.
21. Apollinaire, "Guerre," 160.

22. See McGuinness, *Wittgenstein*, 204.

23. Hayek, *Draft Biography of Ludwig Wittgenstein*.

NOTEBOOK 1: AUGUST 9, 1914–OCTOBER 30, 1914
 1. David Pinsent (1891–1918). See the Introduction.
 2. Bertrand Russell (1872–1970). See the Introduction.

NOTEBOOK 3: MARCH 28 (?), 1916–JANUARY 1, 1917
 1. Monk, *Ludwig Wittgenstein*, 134.

AFTERWORD
 1. BNE, MS. 106, 4, my translation. The manuscript designations here and throughout are those of G. H. von Wright, in his original cataloging of the Wittgenstein papers in the *Nachlass*, which was to be transcribed in the Bergen Electronic Edition. Cited by Somavilla, *Verschlüsselung in Wittgensteins Nachlass*, 367.
 2. See Erbacher, *Wittgenstein's Heirs and Editors*, 2. Author's emphasis.
 3. Wittgenstein, *Philosophical Investigations*.
 4. Erbacher, *Wittgenstein's Heirs and Editors*, 26.
 5. See Somavilla, *Verschlüsselung in Wittgensteins Nachlass*, 371.
 6. Engelmann, *Letters from Ludwig Wittgenstein*, xiv.
 7. See Erbacher, "'Among the Omitted Stuff.'"
 8. See Wittgenstein, *Geheime Tagebücher*; Wittgenstein, *Diari segreti*; Wittgenstein, *Carnets secrets*.
 9. The prominent Wittgenstein scholar David Stern has a scholarly edition under way that will include translation of the full *Notebooks 1914–1916*.
 10. Russell, "Introduction," *Tractatus*, 22.
 11. See, for example, Moi, *Revolution of the Ordinary*; Zumhagen-Yekplé, *A Different Order of Difficulty*.
 12. Monk, *Ludwig Wittgenstein*, 585.
 13. See Monk, *Ludwig Wittgenstein*, 258.
 14. Janik and Toulmin, *Wittgenstein's Vienna*.
 15. Somavilla and Humphries, *Wittgensteins Denkbewegungen*.

BIBLIOGRAPHY

Note: Wittgenstein sources in the Bibliography are listed chronologically by date of original publication.

APOLLINAIRE, GUILLAUME. "Guerre." In *Calligrammes*, translated by Anne Hyde Greet. Berkeley: University of California Press, 1980.

BAUM, WILLIAM. *Wittgenstein im Ersten Weltkrieg: Die "Geheimen Tagebücher" und die Erfahrungen an der Front (1914–1918)*. Klagenfurt, Austria: Kitab Verlag, 2014.

DRURY, M. O'C. "Some Notes on Conversations with Wittgenstein." In *Ludwig Wittgenstein: Personal Recollections*, edited by Rush Rhees, 91–111. Totowa, N.J.: Rowman & Littlefield, 1981.

ENGELMANN, PAUL. *Letters from Ludwig Wittgenstein—With a Memoir*. Oxford: Blackwell, 1967.

ERBACHER, CHRISTIAN. " 'Among the Omitted Stuff, There Are Many Good Remarks of a General Nature'—On the Making of von Wright and Wittgenstein's Culture and Value." *SATS*, 18, no. 2 (2000), https://www.degruyter.com/view/journals/sats/18/2/article-\$29.xml/.

———. *Wittgenstein's Heirs and Editors*. Cambridge, UK: Cambridge University Press, Cambridge Elements online, 2020.

HAYEK, FRIEDRICH VON. *Draft Biography of Ludwig Wittgenstein: The Text and Its History* (English and German ed.), edited by Christian Erbacher. Paderborn, Germany: Mentis, 2019.

JANIK, ALLAN, AND STEPHEN TOULMIN. *Wittgenstein's Vienna*, 2nd ed. Chicago: Ivan R. Dee, 1996.

KUUSELA, OSKARI, AND MARIE McGINN, EDS. *The Oxford Handbook of Witt-genstein.* Oxford: Oxford University Press, 2011.

McGUINNESS, BRIAN. *Wittgenstein, A Life: Young Ludwig 1889–1921.* Berkeley: University of California Press, 1988.

———. "Wittgenstein and Biography." In *The Oxford Handbook of Witt-genstein,* edited by Oskari Kuusela and Marie McGinn, 13–22. Oxford: Oxford University Press, 2011.

McGUINNESS, BRIAN, ED. *Wittgenstein's Family Letters,* translated by Peter Winslow. London: Bloomsbury Academic, 2018.

MOI, TORIL. *Revolution of the Ordinary. Literary Studies after Wittgenstein, Austin, and Cavell.* Chicago: University of Chicago Press, 2017.

MONK, RAY. *Ludwig Wittgenstein: The Duty of Genius.* New York: Macmillan, 1990.

PERLOFF, MARJORIE. *Wittgenstein's Ladder: Poetic Language and the Strangeness of the Ordinary.* Chicago: University of Chicago Press, 1996.

———. *Edge of Irony: Modernism in the Shadow of the Habsburg Empire.* Chicago: University of Chicago Press, 2016.

PILCH, MARTIN. "Wittgenstein's 'Gebetsstriche' in den Kriegstgebüchern (MSS. 101–103)." In *Aesthetics Today,* Contemporary Approaches to the Aesthetics of Nature and of Art (39th International Wittgenstein Symposium, Kirchberg am Wechsel, August 2016), edited by Stefan Majetschak and Anja Weiberg, 192–95, https://www.alws.at/alws/wp-$2ntent/uploads/2019/01/papers-$216.pdf.

———. "Die Entstehung des Tractatus im 1 Weltkrieg—Nachträge zur Biographie." In *Ludwig Wittgenstein: Die Tractatus Odyssee,* edited by Radmila Schweitzer.

———. "März-September 1916: Ludwig Wittgenstein während der Brussilow-Offensive in der Bukovina." In *Ludwig Wittgenstein: Die Tractatus Odyssee,* edited by Radmila Schweitzer.

SCHWEITZER, RADMILA, ED. *Ludwig Wittgenstein: Die Tractatus Odyssee.* Wien: Wittgenstein Initiative, 2018.

SLUGA, HANS, AND DAVID G. Stern, eds. *The Cambridge Companion to Witt-genstein,* 2nd ed. Cambridge, UK: Cambridge University Press, 2017.

SOMAVILLA, ILSE. *Verschlüsselung in Wittgensteins Nachlass.* Publications of the Austrian Ludwig Wittgenstein Society—New Series, vol. 14, 366–86. Innsbruck: Ontos Verlag, 2002.

SOMAVILLA, ILSE, AND CARL HUMPHRIES. *Wittgensteins Denkbewegungen (Tagebücher 1930–32 / 1936–37), Interdisciplinary Perspectives.* Innsbruck, Wien, Bozen: Studien Verlag, 2019.

STERN, DAVID G. "The Availability of Wittgenstein's Philosophy." In *The Cambridge Companion to Wittgenstein*, 2nd ed., edited by Hans Sluga and David G. Stern, 442–76. Cambridge, UK: Cambridge University Press, 2017.

TOLSTOY, LEO. *The Gospel in Brief: The Life of Jesus*, translated by Dustin Condren. New York: Harper, 2011.

VON WRIGHT, G. H. "Biographical Sketch." In Norman Malcolm, *Ludwig Wittgenstein: A Memoir, with a Biographical Sketch by G. H. von Wright and Wittgenstein's Letters to Malcolm*, 2nd ed., 1–20. Oxford: Oxford University Press, 1984.

WITTGENSTEIN, HERMINE. "My Brother Ludwig." In *Ludwig Wittgenstein: Personal Recollections*, edited by Rush Rhees. Totowa, N.J.: Rowman & Littlefield, 1984.

WITTGENSTEIN, LUDWIG. *Notebooks 1914–1916*, 2nd ed., edited by G. H. von Wright and G. E. M. Anscombe, translated by G. E. M. Anscombe. Chicago: University of Chicago Press, 1979.

———. *Tractatus Logico-Philosophicus*, bilingual ed., translated by C. K. Ogden, with an Introduction by Bertrand Russell. London: Routledge, 1992. (Originally published 1922.)

———. *The Blue and Brown Books*, 2nd ed., edited by Rush Rhees. New York: Harper, 1960.

———. *Philosophical Investigations*, bilingual ed., translated by G. E. M. Anscombe, P. M. S. Hacker, and Joachim Schulte. Revised 4th ed. by P. M. S. Hacker and Joachim Schulte. Oxford: Wiley-Blackwell, 2009.

———. *Lectures and Conversations on Aesthetics, Psychology, and Religious Belief*, edited by Cyril Barrett. Berkeley: University of California Press, 2007.

———. *Culture and Value*, rev. ed., edited by G. H. von Wright; revised edition of the text by Alois Pichler. Translated by Peter Winch. Oxford: Blackwell, 1998.

———. *Zettel*, bilingual ed., edited by G. E. M. Anscombe and G. H. Wright. Berkeley: University of California Press, 1967.

————. *Wittgenstein's Lectures Cambridge, 1930–32*. From the Notes of John King and Desmond Lee, edited by Desmond Lee. Chicago: University of Chicago Press, 1980.

————. *Carnets secrets 1914–1916*, translated by Jean-Pierre Cometti. Paris: Farrago, 2001.

————. *Diari segreti*, translated by Fabrizio Funtò, with an Introduction by Aldo G. Gargani. Bari, Italy: Laterza, 1987.

————. *Diarios secretos*. Madrid: Alianza Universidad, 1991.

————. *Geheime Tagebücher 1914–1916*, edited by William Baum. Wien: Turia & Kant, 1991.

————. *Briefe. Briefwechsel mit B. Russell, G. E. Moore, J. M. Keynes, F. P. Ramsey, W. Eccles, P. Engelmann, L. von Ficker*, edited by B. F. McGuinness and G. H. von Wright. Frankfurt: Suhrkamp, 1980.

ZUMHAGEN-YEKPLÉ, KAREN. *A Different Order of Difficulty: Literature After Wittgenstein*. Chicago: University of Chicago Press, 2020.

ARCHIVES

WITTGENSTEIN, LUDWIG. Wittgenstein's Nachlass: The Bergen Electronic Edition, edited by Wittgenstein Archives at the University of Bergen under the direction of Claus Huitfeldt. Oxford: Oxford University Press, 2000. This edition cited as BEE.

————. Wittgenstein Source Bergen Nachlass Edition, edited by Wittgenstein Archives at the University of Bergen under the direction of Alois Pichler. Wittgenstein Source (2009–), http://wittgensteinsource.org. Bergen: University of Bergen, 2015–. This edition is cited as BNE.

————. Interactive Dynamic Presentation (IDP) of *Ludwig Wittgenstein's Philosophical Nachlass*, edited by Wittgenstein Archives at the University of Bergen under the direction of Alois Pichler, http://wittgensteinonline.no/. Bergen: University of Bergen, 2016.

————. *Wittgenstein Collection*. Research Institute, Brenner Archive, University of Innsbruck, Austria (n.d.).

ABOUT THE AUTHOR
AND THE TRANSLATOR

LUDWIG WITTGENSTEIN (1889–1951), widely regarded as the most important philosopher of the twentieth century, was born into one of the wealthiest—and highly cultured—families in Vienna. His family roots were Jewish but he was brought up as a Catholic. Trained as an engineer, he never formally studied philosophy, but as a young man, studying aeronautics in England, Wittgenstein came across Bertrand Russell's *Principia Mathematica* and decided to study logic with Russell at Cambridge. Pupil quickly became master, and Wittgenstein's first book, the *Tractatus Logico-Philosophicus* (1922), composed largely during active combat on the Eastern Front during World War I, presents a radical counterargument on logic that concludes with "mystical" speculations on ethics, aesthetics, and religion. It was in the *Tractatus* that Wittgenstein declared *"The limits of my language* mean the limits of my world," the mystery of how language works soon becoming his central preoccupation.

After the war, Wittgenstein gave away his entire fortune and worked for six years as a primary school teacher in the impoverished villages of lower Austria. In 1929, having become something of a celebrity for the *Tractatus*, Wittgenstein accepted an invitation from Cambridge to teach philosophy. He made his primary home there until his death in 1951. But although he lectured in English, he continued to write in German and considered himself an exile in a somewhat alien world. His aphoristic and often poetic writings, many now classics, such as *Culture and Value*, have been published in bilingual editions, as accessible in his native Austria and Germany as in the Anglophone world.

From the *Tractatus* to his most widely read book, the *Philosophical Investigations*, published in 1953 shortly after his death, Wittgenstein was committed to the idea that philosophy is not a set of theories but an *activity*—the activity of taking on the basic philosophical questions to which there can never be a satisfactory answer. Suspicious of all abstraction and generalization and eager to turn philosophy away from the dominance of science in the modern world, Wittgenstein taught us not *what* to think but *how* to think, all the while insisting that philosophy needs no metalanguage, that "ordinary language is alright."

———

MARJORIE PERLOFF was born Gabriele Mintz in Vienna and emigrated, with her refugee family, to New York in 1938. Raised bilingually, she is the author of many books including *Wittgenstein's Ladder: Poetic Language and the Strangeness of the Ordinary*; *Edge of Irony: Modernism in the Shadow of the Habsburg Empire*; and a memoir, *The Vienna Paradox*. She has written widely and lectured around the world on modern and avant-garde poetry and poetics: Her most recent book is *Infrathin: An Experiment in Micropoetics* (2021). Until her retirement, she taught English and Comparative Literature at Stanford University and at the University of Southern California.